A Feast Of Life

Living Humbly and Full Of Vegetables

By Mrs. Kate Singh

Katesinghwrites.blog

Goodreads.com/katesingh7

Copyright @ 2024 by Kate Singh. All rights reserved. No portion of this book may be reproduced without written permission from the publisher or author except as permitted by U.S. copyright law.

Table Of Contents

Chapter One: A Simple and Affordable Life

Chapter Two: Our Sanctuary of Used and Free

Chapter Three: Our Most Important Assets

Chapter Four: A Happy Mind Is Free And Invaluable

Chapter Five: Old Cars Or On Foot

Chapter Six: Our Humble But Luxurious Life

Chapter Seven: A Scratch Kitchen

Chapter Eight: Building A Sanctuary By Hand

Chapter Nine: No More Over Working And Burn Out

Chapter Ten: Affording The Gift Of Staying Home

Chapter Eleven: Do I Get Bored At Home?

Chapter Twelve: The End Of Poverty Consciousness

Chapter One

A Simple and Affordable Life.

Welcome to my life and home. If you were here, I'd brew some coffee and prepare a plate of delectables, maybe dates and fruits, cheeses, and homemade crackers. I've gone back to plant-based eating, but I wouldn't make you suffer from vegan cheeses, although there are some good ones out there now, maybe some herbed vegan cream cheeses. We'd have coffee with extra creamy oat milk and date syrup, a couple of shots of espresso from a little green espresso machine I found free, still new and in the box on the street a couple of Summers ago. If you were here specifically to learn some tricks on frugality, you might have come to me because you wanted to quit your job and be at home for children, start making pottery in your garage, or write a novel; in that case, I'd show you everything from all the furniture and art I've found free, to the pantry filled with rice and beans. I would show you the closets of nice clothes from garage sales and the **Make Your Grocery** cookbooks. We would stroll in the small orchard and look over the garden and the side kitchen garden. If it was Summer or a nice day, we would sit on the patio near the pool or on the large porch and have iced tea. I would have Opera or Blue Grass playing in the background and insist you stay for Supper, which is always a fine little feast. We'd have a blast, and you would, hopefully, leave inspired and armed with good ideas and hope.

Many of you know me through many books I've written because I can't talk enough about this life of abundance and easy living or from my old YouTube channel. I no longer have the channel and chose to take the videos down, but that is for another little talk. Some of you will be new, and I hope you enjoy this book and that it enriches your life.

Recently, I deleted my videos and took a break from YouTube. It was nothing negative, just that my kids called on me to be more present and less preoccupied with filming. I also felt guided to refocus on my writing. I am, specifically, getting back to fiction. So, I quit my job. This is always a little nerve-wracking because I have to stretch that one income a lot. I haven't written a book in almost two years, so my passive income from book royalties is small, but it makes ends meet a bit easier. My husband works as a cashier at a gas station. We are in California, so the minimum wage is higher than in other states, but so is everything else. We have some of the highest rents, gas, groceries, and housing market prices. Boo Hoo for us, but we are clever and have learned how to live well despite it all.

I remember a section in **The Complete Tightwad Gazette** where Amy Dacyczyn talks about having a second income and the pros and cons. In the end, she suggested that in some situations, it's wisest to stay home and find ways to save money instead of being gone all the time and having most of your earnings go to taxes, commuting, daycare, and so on. I wasn't working outside the home, but my channel did take a lot of time away from writing, resting, and focusing on the kids. It took time and thought daily. When I was done filming, I often didn't have the energy to write. Having a channel was terrific, and I had a beautiful community that I miss terribly. Still, sometimes, we need to step away from one situation or career to focus on something else. Sometimes, we must give up one thing to have something else. I wanted to say yes to the most precious things. Yes to my family and yes to writing, thus, I had to say no to everything else. And it has paid off big time. But we will get into that later.

Now that the focus is on family and my home, everyone benefits. I've been getting much-needed rest and reading good books. My writing magic has returned, and I have found many ways to save money on our utilities and groceries. I've been painting rooms, beautifying my home, and helping the kids with schoolwork. We are all thriving. As I sit here doing the last edit, we have just returned from a two-hour walk and bike ride on a forest trail that leads to a small shopping center. I needed vegan sour cream, and the kids wanted a bike ride. My little dog needed to be worn out, or she sits at my feet and stares at me.

My little dog, Molly, who was so plump she looked like a massive loaf of bread on tiny feet, is now slimmed down because I'm focused on her diet of fresh vegetables and turkey neck I get at the butcher's for very little money. She and I go for long walks almost daily. She is fit and slim at last. I had two elder dogs, but they have passed in the last few seasons. So, Molly gets all the attention now.

I have turned back to plant-based food, making 85% of everything fresh and organic, with plenty of raw fruits and vegetables. I have found all sorts of workout equipment for free or on sale to create a home gym, and we are slowly getting healthy and fit.

We get the bills paid on time, but we have to be thoughtful with everything, such as using the solar wisely, not heating the whole house when gone, using natural lighting during the day, using more crock pot cooking, and less baking with gas. I know every trick in the book and use them all now.

I'm also currently working on three books. And that was the whole idea. I would stop working on a channel and focus on writing and educating myself. We would live lean in the meantime, and hopefully, I will have that time to find my writing voice.

This is all because I narrowed the focus to family and writing.

This idea of going to a more spartan existence and needing less money started a few years ago when I read **Essentialism** by Greg McKeown and realized I had taken on too much and was working myself into the ground. I was tired and grumpy. I felt guilty about not focusing on my little kids as much. I was irritable because I had so much on my plate daily. But this was my doing and all my fault. I make life like that. I pile my plate high and don't realize my limits. When we lived on a fruit farm, almost ten years ago, I didn't work. I tended to the home and babies, cooked simple casseroles, played music in the house, and read novels to pass the time. It was lovely back then. I was calm, peaceful, nurturing, and motherly like a saint.

But I was afraid to give up my hustles because I was pulling in a decent amount of income each month, and we were used to the extra money. Our new mortgage was $500 more than the last mortgage, and I like to shop just like the next person. We had plenty of money to order what we needed, used books and music, and plenty of groceries. I was concerned and felt I needed these jobs. At the time, I had a channel on YouTube, a blog, and Patreon. Then, I had the book royalties, and I was whipping up a book and publishing it every few months. This is too much work for a woman who is also a 1950s-style housewife, keeping a lovely home, cooking, cleaning, working on our fixer-upper, and gardening. And the biggest job of all: raising boys and homeschooling. So, all my work was passable.

Barely. Luke warm and mediocre. And I was thinking I was going through perimenopause. Maybe I was, maybe not. I sure don't feel that way anymore. I feel wonderful.

It was a memory of a woman I have discussed in books before, but she is worth discussing again, and that snapped me out of my money fears. In my twenties, I stayed with a friend for two months. She was a single mother living in these cheap, tan apartments on the edge of town. Across from her was her friend, who we'll call Doreen, who had an apartment upstairs above the carport. She was single, raising two tweens, and had decided that instead of working two or three jobs and never being around, thus having her girls on their own and being latchkey kids and running around with who knows who, getting into trouble, she would go to college. There was only a community college, but it was only a few miles from her apartment, and the campus was beautiful, loaded with classes, and offered all sorts of degrees. My memory is vague, but I know she didn't work. She didn't have time. She took 16 to 20 units a semester, almost double a full load (a full class load was 12 units). I would visit her, and there would be stacks of books open and spread out on the table, the old computer (this was the days of the big, square box of a computer) was on, coffee brewing, and she would be in the middle of writing papers and studying for a test. She had no money. I remember her counting out change for gas for her old beast of a car that was kept together with wire and tape. I also remember going to a warehouse to get government rations. This was thirty years ago when food banks handed out government blocks of cheese, bags of rice, and beans. Despite being as broke as possible, she loved school, which gave her such a purpose. She was always home when her girls got out of school. She was there for their games, there to bake brownies for bake sales, and she was there for all school dances and meetings. She was there for all parts of their awkward tweens and teens. And she was improving her family's life, one semester at a time.

She finished college in a few years with a couple of degrees and got a job working in one of the departments at the college. She even retired from there. She did well financially, bought a little cottage, and had a good life. I know this because my old friend stayed friends with her, and I was updated now and then on Doreen's life.

So, I recalled this period, and this mother, and it made me think that maybe it wouldn't be so bad to be broke for a little bit if I had a purpose. I love writing; it runs in my veins, as does coffee. I have never thought, "I need a break from writing" or "I'm burnt out from writing; I need to retire." No, I've never thought a molecule of a negative or tiring thing about writing. I love to write, whether I'm good or not; it is my second love. The children are my first, and writing is second. So, I knew I had to figure things out and let everything go that wasn't my children or my writing. I had to focus if I wanted to succeed at something truly. You never get a second chance at your kid's childhood. They grow up, and that is that. You can't write well if you are trying to do fifty other projects.

It has taken a few years to downsize my "To Do" list, but here we sit, and I'm a mother and writer. Nothing else is on the list.

Every penny is put to hard work. Bills are paid immediately or ahead of time. The vehicle's tanks are filled with gas, and we drive as little as possible. When I have money for groceries, I buy 50 lbs. of organic pintos and brown rice (the cheapest of all beans and rice), wheat pastry flour (also the cheapest of flours), and all-purpose flour. I will stock up on frozen fruits and vegetables at Grocery Outlet and plant milk and creamers. Then, WinCo for bulk seasonings, nutritional yeast, nuts, organic white rice, popcorn, coffee, and odds and ends for scratch cooking. We buy organic produce from the health food store at the same price or cheaper than Grocery Outlet every ten days to two weeks. I go to our local food pantry every other week and only take the produce, plant milk, and bread bags. They throw in a vegetarian bag since I have us listed as a vegetarian family. We get some exciting things in there, maybe Lightlife vegan ground, tofu, health bars, vegan snacks.

We grow food now. We have just started growing food successfully, but we will only have more success each year. I have all the equipment and skills to preserve our harvest by dehydrating and canning.

I no longer worry about money. We have all we need. But we did have to buy a cheap house, as cheap as you can get in California and this area, and we have old cars that are paid for and no debt or credit cards. This is the only way to live a cheap life. But a cheap life means an easy life. It means *time* for life. It means we can be happy and enjoy the simplest gifts of life.

The other day, I was waiting in the car line at the food pantry. The car in front of me was a male version of me. He drove an old, dented, faded car with a cracked windshield. He read what was probably a library book while waiting. He was probably wearing thrift finds. It warmed the cockles of my heart. He may look down and out to the untrained eye, but to me, I see a life of contentment. A life that has stepped out of worldly things and is at peace. We may look poor, but I feel middle class, even through my cracked windshield. I have all the joys of life. We have a warm, bohemian home. We have soft beds. We eat good food because I can make all kinds of delicious dishes with essential ingredients, and I'm obsessed with vegan cooking channels. We dress well because I hunt and scavenge for nice clothing, visit thrift stores during big sales, find clothes at garage sales, and buy boxes full for a twenty spot. I found a box of clothes yesterday when I took Molly for a walk. There were new boots for Sam, and I now have a gorgeous soft pink sweater, a long-striped, stretchy dress, and many other items that round out my wardrobe. All free. We have Roku TV, which means hundreds of thousands of good movies and shows. Free. I'm reading a few delightful books from the library: *The Invisible Woman* **and** *Mrs. Jordan's Profession; The Actress and the Prince*, both by Claire Tomalin, and *Farm City; The Education Of An Urban Farmer* by Novella Carpenter. There is also a stack of movies I'm working on as I fold laundry and write this.

Some people are impoverished, and the struggle is daily. We are fortunate not to be in that situation. I met a woman in the little forest by our house today. She and I chatted. She was very nice but told tall tales. I have learned from having a dear friend who developed a mental illness and wound-up living in her car that one of the first things people learn on the streets is how to tell a lie and weave stories without blinking an eye. It's how they survive, camp somewhere for a time, get away from cops, or get what they need to make it daily. So, this lovely lady says she left her bike in the woods. I asked if she felt safe retrieving it alone because somebody's tent had been set up for maybe a month. She and I discussed that it seemed abandoned, and then she was on her way. When I came back around on the outskirts of the trail, I saw she was messing with the tent, and I realized she lived there. She also said her boyfriend had died a while back of congestive heart disease, but my neighbor, seeing me across the street talking to this woman, called me and said he was alive and walking the streets all the time. This woman is just trying to survive in her life. I would not wish it on anyone.

There are so many reasons people are homeless or struggling. Rents are awful in California, and I don't know how people make them. I don't have advice on surviving paying rent that takes up 70% of your income. I read a book once, Evicted: Poverty And Profit In An American City, by Matthew Desmond, and he covered a handful of situations where people were trying to make it and failing. There were families and single people who were all going through evictions and struggling to remain sheltered. Some lived in a trailer park, and some lived in slum apartments. There were many reasons, from years of poor choices and drug addiction to wrong partners and bad landlords.

Not enough money is a problem. So can too much money be a problem.

In one recent interview, I watched a little thing on Jim Carrey, in which he announced he was retiring from Hollywood; he said, "I have enough, I've done enough, I am enough." He said he liked his quiet life and his spiritual life.

Times are tough, but they've always been challenging, with brief moments of grandeur. The Roaring Twenties were before the crushing Great Depression and the housing boom before the recession of 2008. There are more examples I can't think of right now, but the economy goes up and down constantly. Riding through the rough parts depends on how we prepare during the golden times. What do we do during prosperous times? That will dictate how we manage through the recessions and depressions.

We also have to consider if we are on incomes that are set and limited, such as disability and welfare. If we work, it all depends on how much we work, where we work, if we take on another side hustle, if we do something to generate income from home, such as being an influencer on YouTube or other outlets, or maybe we knit or bake and sell our products, write books, blog, or garden and sell produce from our yard. I feel like there is always a way to make extra money. However, as Amy Dacyczyn said in the introduction of her Complete Tightwad Gazette, "If you want more money, you can either find a higher paying job, or you can save more money." Many of her readers have had success following the latter of the two options. Also, this is in her words. Her advice has been criticized for being too extreme, but she says that this is how a family *does* make it on a small income. She said it takes creativity and discipline, and she mentions that most mainstream frugal advisors stay in a "safe zone" and talk about how impossible it is to make it on even two incomes. Well, our frugal heroine suggests that it *would* be impossible to get by living in the safe frugal zone and that only practicing extreme measures will help a family survive and even thrive on a small income.

I don't do the extreme frugality. Yet. I have TCTWG out right now, and I'm rereading it front to back just like I did when the boys were wee babes, and I had the husband bring home a small paycheck for me to stretch. I couldn't work if I wanted to because we lived far from a big town and had only one car. I didn't want to do another daycare or babysit. Hey, I didn't want to work, period. I had babies I'd waited all my life for and wanted to enjoy homemaking and being a mother. So, as you guessed, I had to be super impressive with the money. I could have done better, but we did just fine.

Today, I am older and still raising kids and tending to a home. I have done side gigs and at-home hustles. I have brought in a nice side paycheck to help us get ahead, but it turns out that being self-employed, so much of what I made went to taxes. Not a waste, but I heard Amy's words echo in my mind, and I decided that in 2024, I would learn how to save more and work less. After all, I want to love my home and family and write books without the pressure to succeed. As writers, we never know what a hit will be or if we will ever have one. Writing must be a pleasure and from the heart.

I had a high school friend who married and had a child at seventeen. Her life was not easy after that. Her first house was a tiny, itsy bitsy one-bedroom. I remember her making meals from big boxes of Minute rice and bags of frozen chicken breast. Her family was not the healthiest; they made a lot of premade and prepackaged foods. She only knew how to cook simple things. She did a lot of tuna and crackers as well. She married and divorced twice and had two kids. She had a daycare for years and did a lot of odd jobs, but at one point, she was on welfare and food stamps. This was back when the amount of food stamps was small. She had all the government assistance one could have, and she was very fortunate to have this, but it is a limited amount, so smarts and tricks are necessary. I wish I had paid more attention, but I remember much of what she did. I have talked about her many times, but I'll share again.

We will call her Bernice. I used to call her Miss B, but I read a frugal book recently with Miss B in it, so let's choose a new name for her. Bernice has passed since; she had been sick a long time, so working was out for her. She worked with what she had. She had an old house that had been her home with her ex-husband, but the landlords turned it into a Section 8 house for her later, which was a huge blessing. I don't remember her receiving any money from the ex-husband, so she had to stretch the welfare and food stamps. She would shop at FoodMaxx, and that woman could load up on groceries for just $50. She was conservative with the water and electricity. She lived on coffee, always had a pot brewing, and often bought the cheapest stuff, dark roast Maxwell House. I remember the blue container on her counter. She made a lot of premixed things like powdered biscuits that didn't require eggs, oil, or milk. That does help when you are tight on funds. She had old furniture people had given her but covered recliners and couches with her grandmother's Afghans to cover the wear. Her grandmother's paintings were on the wall, and she used area rugs to cover the old linoleum in the kitchen and bathroom. She spent time shopping shrewdly at thrift stores where she found .25 cent t-shirts and .10 candles. She loved having a candle glowing on the table or her side stand by the recliner she would rest in. People gave her their old Readers Digest and magazines; her parents would get her turkeys and ham when the two-for-one deals were happening. On church days, she could enjoy free coffee and donuts. Her family was heavily involved with the church, and she would buy bags of clothes for a couple of dollars during flea markets. And I'm sure the church helped her occasionally. Her parents were big Costco shoppers, so they would get her supplies like tissue or soap. After the holidays, Bernice would start hitting all the big sales, stocking up on her baking supplies and stocking stuffers, and storing them all in bins under her bed. She was always hunting and mastering sales. She knew when to get 80% sales and when the hospice thrift shop had deals. I have never found .25-cent shirts, and I'm always shocked by what thrift stores charge for used candles. But she was the queen of sales and finds.

Her house was always scrubbed clean, she always had excellent food spreads on the table during the holidays, and she always had a pot of coffee brewing. She also would find cheap scented lotions and have them in the bathroom. She dressed in clean clothes without stains and holes. They may be simple outfits of t-shirts, shorts, and flip-flops, but they were ironed and fresh-looking. She had fantastic hair, eyelashes, and lips, and she would pile her hair up, put the mascara on thick, and always had lip gloss and scented lotion. Her makeup and hair dye were from Dollar Tree or Grocery Outlet. She wore big earrings, and her finger and toe nails were always painted. It doesn't cost a lot to look good.

When we had money pouring in, and there were abundant times, especially during the quarantine with the stimulus checks, I prepared for the lean times. I had some foresight and knew I'd wind down with all the work. I had a vision of me not always busy and pulling in money. We took the extra money and planted gardens and orchards. We stocked up on garden tools, a huge Berkey water filter, kitchen tools, fencing, and other materials for DIY home projects. We found a cheap above-ground pool—books, clothes, and music. We built everything we needed to build, such as a second bathroom, a patio, and a pergola. We rebuilt the foundation. We paid off all our little debts. We also saved an emergency fund. The pantry is stocked, and the toiletries and cleaning stuff are too. We also did all the tune-ups, replaced the coils, brakes, and filters, and did all the repairs on the truck and car.

So, this helps us get by on much less. We receive a nice refund every year, and we can break it into monthly allotments to get through the year. We didn't have to do this before, but now it is a safety net with our small earnings. If we do it smartly, we will have plenty of money for groceries and bills for a year until the following tax refund. Or an emergency fund.

How simple and inexpensive you want to make life is your business. It is between you and your family. Hopefully, they will be on board. Mine is on board, but why wouldn't they be? Life is good, and mom is always home to wipe away tears, join in laughs and silliness, reprimand lousy behavior, and monitor computer time. They probably aren't crazy about the last part. Then there are all the homemade meals, baked goods, and the comfort of having mom there.

I think of two extremes because I've studied all simple and humble living levels. There is frugal living for a better life, and then there is a frugal obsession and can steal joy. There are also different levels of living "poor" that work for different souls.

A couple of years back, I read a book called The *Man Who Quit Money* by Mark Sundeen. It's about a real-life man named Daniel Suelo, a man who had worked in social services and had been of service for most of his life, who became disgusted with the whole energy around money, how it was used, abused, the greed, the lack and the government services, the way people were with their money and the politics and corruption dealing with money. He walked away from his last few dollars one day and successfully lived for almost 20 years without dealing with money again. It is a fascinating story. He continued to be of service in many ways, volunteering at battered women's shelters, coop gardens, food banks, and soup kitchens. He was able to feed himself by eating at the soup kitchens where he worked and getting produce given to him from gardens where he would volunteer. He dumpster dived, found roadkill, foraged for herbs and roots, berries and nuts, or enjoyed harvest left behind in fields to rot. He never asks for money or even to exchange work for things, food, and such. He wanted everything to be offered and given without obligation. Even his volunteer work was never from obligation or needing something in return. He was surrounded by friends and community, some of whom he started online as he journaled his thoughts and life in a blog. He had enough to eat and lived in hidden caves. He didn't trash or disrespect the natural places he took shelter. He was careful to tread lightly and respect nature.

There was a Native American Chief who said the key to living on less was reducing one's needs.

Not all of us could or would want to live like this. But it is fascinating how much we could strip down and still thrive. Maybe not so much with kids in tow.

Another example is a movie about a coach who moves his family to a tiny, dusty, almost abandoned town to coach at a high school. **MacFarland USA**, with Kevin Costner. It's based on a true story of this coach taking some lost boys and making them into runners and how they change him for the better. At some point in the movie, the coach is offered a great job at a private school in the Bay Area. His kids would go to this private school all paid, his salary would be significant, benefits, retirement, and they would move back to an affluent and friendly area. But his wife didn't want to leave. He didn't feel his girls were safe there because there were small gangs and drama at times, but his wife felt the girls were safer there than anywhere because they had become close to the Hispanic community, which watched over all of them like family. It was more community and family than they had experienced in the cities, suburbs, and upper class. She felt it was their home. It was a dusty town that was forgotten, their house was not great, and the education wasn't stellar, but they had community and a reason to be there. So, they stayed, and incredible things happened that rippled into the next generations.

Some of us may have taken that job with the private school and more upper-crust town, but there is something about that feeling of home and belonging. It can't be replaced with an excellent salary and a retirement safety net. Money doesn't make us warm and safe. It gives us things and can be used for good and genuine comfort, but we never know where or how we will find the ultimate: home, family, community, and service.

Chapter Two

Our Sanctuary Of Used and Free

We do own a home in California. This state is outrageous regarding housing costs and rents, and the worst part is a significant shortage of houses. According to an article I found online by Travis Schlepp on KTLA5 California News, *only 7 million of California's roughly 40 million residents own their homes.* To add more to a depressing statistic, there are only 14 million housing units. This article was in 2023, so perhaps there are more now. Surprisingly, we are one of the 7 million people who own a house. We are the least likely to own a house. We make very little, although we made $42,000 that year when we bought this house. Ah, but we had to work so very hard that year. Bali worked doubles four days a week and a part-time job on the weekends. I wrote and published book after book and filmed for a YouTube channel almost daily, along with blogging daily. We worked far too much only to have scrapped together this $42,000, but when you write homemaking books, your channel is small, and your husband works at a gas station for $14 an hour, you work hard and live small.

And living small is what made it possible to buy this house. I bartered for an old house, and we rented out the little house we owned then because we couldn't sell it that year. That worked out great. It showed an extra income and made it all possible. Later, after a year, the housing cost went up again, and we sold the old rental and made a profit that we used to pay off half of this house. At one point, we owned two houses in a state where only 7 million people own a house. We are unlikely candidates for this sort of prosperity in property.

The only way we have a house is because we have no debt. Let me be clear: we incur some debt occasionally, but we pay it off quickly, within months. Paupers such as us could never afford a house in a nice area if we had car payments or credit cards. It is a delicate balance, for sure. When you ask for a loan, the " debt-to-earnings ratio is first analyzed." So, we keep that clear. We have a Home Depot card and run it up when deep in home repairs and improvements, but we then work double time to pay it off before any interest can be collected. I feel credit cards are unnecessary; I have money set aside. We have this card because Bali likes having it, so I keep it tucked away for those emergency repairs.

We have owned two houses in the last seven years. It took forever to buy the first. I was 46 or 47 when we owned our first home. It was $135,000 for a dirty, 1940s stucco house that had sheltered many a squatter over the years. I bid for this HUD house, and since no one else bid that day, by midnight, it was ours. We scrubbed, soaped, boiled, and painted it back to an adorable cottage. In tearing out the stained, molded carpet, we found lovely old wood floors and oiled them liberally. We dug up the overgrown yards, planted fruit and nut trees, and put in kitchen gardens. After reading *Novella Carpenter's* book, *Farm City*, I learned of the value of horse manure, so Bali and I would drive out to the country and fill the truck with horse manure from a vast pile kept outside a horse ranch that was free to anyone. It was a game changer; our garden produced ample veggies and fruits after a couple of truckloads.

A few years later, I was determined to move us up the mountain to a forest town loaded with history and Victorian-lined streets. Everything was there for my family: hiking trails, a small, quaint town, and enlightened schools. I woke up one morning and received the message that we had a year to make it happen, or it was game over. Bali and I worked like dogs and saved every penny. We ate from our kitchen gardens, hung the laundry outside, cooked from scratch, and stocked the pantry with 50 lb. bags of rice, beans, and oats. We didn't shop or buy anything outside of groceries. At the time, I had generous subscribers from a YouTube channel who would send WinCo cards or money. I used every penny wisely to pay off the last little debts and stock the pantry. We lived on $1600 to $1800 a month and sometimes less. Our mortgage was much smaller then.

I won't bore you with the gory details, but we spent the whole year saving, working overtime, and searching for that home. We were outbid, denied, and one time, we just threw in the towel because the house was becoming too much work preparing for an inspection, and we didn't know how we had gotten roped into patching up the place by the realtor. You live and learn. This house we have now, which I named Arthur, was the last somewhat in our price range, and the clock was ticking toward the end of that year. The house was on the market for $289K, which was NOT our price range, but when I explored the yard, all I could see was a big, empty backyard canvas. It was just weeds and gravel, but I saw the future, and the future had a huge organic garden and a small orchard. Then, there was a long, wide porch, and I saw a lot of coffee drinking-and book-reading on that porch. The house was within walking distance of town and many wooded trails. The kids were already in homeschooling charter schools in that town, and I belonged to the food coop. We had been "acting as if" for a couple of years by shopping and schooling up there once a week, and coming up to have play dates on the trails.

I asked the realtor, a mom at one of the forest schools we attended, "What's the lowest I should bid?" She said, "I wouldn't go lower than $260K". I said, "Offer $240K". She cringed but carried out the mission. The owner rejected that bid. At the same time, I discovered we had been denied on a straw bale house we had been waiting to hear from on a short sale, and I was running out of time. I offered $250K and said it was the final offer, take it or leave it, but I needed an answer by that day. I used to get so emotional and cry with a tissue box close by every time we lost a house, but now I was hardened and all business. I just had to make something happen, and soon. I had a signed agreement by that afternoon, and we had Arthur by the end of the month. And true to the prophecy, we moved our last truck load up at precisely the end of a year, and the next day, the world shut down and asked us to remain in our homes to sit out COVID-19. After being locked in our homes for a time, the housing market shot through the roof, and we would *never* have been able to afford a house up here if we had waited.

I listen to my guides always. They're never wrong.

So, don't be afraid to bid low. The realtors will never tell you how low you can go because they only register the commission. Why would they shoot themselves in the foot, right? And don't overlook the old homes. Our sweet Arthur is now 123 years old. He is solid and built with old timber wood. He has been insulated over the years, which was fantastic because the old houses can be very cold because they lack insulation. We had to redo the foundation because there wasn't much of one, but we just redid the post and pier by setting up cement bases and trimming off the bottom rot on the old timber post. We had to bomb the house initially, and recently, we had to respray under the house for wood termites.

Because of rats, we had to replace central heating and air vents. Everything else was for our delight, such as painting the rooms and replacing the floors. We left the old linoleum in the kitchen, pantry, and bathroom, but unfortunately, the rugs were awful, and the old floors underneath were too damaged. We replaced them with bamboo flooring because it was on a huge blowout sale at Home Depot. I wouldn't suggest bamboo; it doesn't age that well.

With some old houses, the bones are strong, but they need some fixing up, and if you are somewhat handy, it can be done slowly over time. The only thing you can't change is the neighborhood.

Chapter Three

Our Most Important Assets

I'm chubby and have struggled with sugar addiction forever. Sugar is more addictive than cocaine. They did a test with lab rats that were addicted to cocaine, and when offered a choice of cocaine or sugar, they chose sugar. For most of my life, I've chosen sugar.

Recently, I returned to the plant-based business. I wanted to try Raw Vegan to cleanse and detox on a deep level. I've polluted my body for years; thus, I'm overweight. You can see how someone has treated their body and what they put in it just by giving them a brief visual scan. We have lumpy, soft bodies, and that says that we have taken in a lot of processed foods and sat on our couches, entertained by the phone or Netflix for more hours than we have walked the roads.

The diet industry is a billion-dollar business. So is sickness. Big Pharma sells pills that don't work, and they make money for it. The diet industry sells diets that starve us, make us miserable, and fail, and they make money for it. The pills don't work; they lead to more pills. I saw this with my mother. She smoked and drank and lived off fried eggs and sausage. Still, the doctors just gave her pills, not a solution or better diet, no way to get off the cigarettes and wine, just more pills that led to more pills. One pill would cause issues with her kidneys, then she needed a pill for water retention, then the liver was getting affected, and there was a pill for that, then the skin, the blood pressure, there was a pill for everything. By the time my mother passed, she had a salad bowl on the table filled with pills that she couldn't keep straight. "Did I already take that yellow one? And have I had the second pink one?" We would get so confused. I genuinely believe that if she had quit smoking and drinking and switched from eggs and sausage to fruit and tofu, she may not have had that massive bowl of pills, and she probably would have seen 90 years.

I'm no doctor, but I suggest reading *How Not To Die by Dr. Greger* or *The China Study by Thomas Campbell.* Suppose books aren't your thing, try *Forks Over Knives* the documentary. There are many documentaries about plant-based living. You can find information on Netflix or YouTube. I know the Keto diet is popular, but people like Dr. Mercola, who made it so famous, now say it wasn't such a great idea. It turns out it's not suitable for women; it takes some years off our lifespan. It is sad to think that a doctor raves about a diet he's not even sure about, and flocks of souls run out and restock their kitchens and follow it faithfully because "Dr. so and so said it was great for us!" How about we start reading and researching for ourselves? Now, if you aren't so hip with the plant-based and can't imagine a life without some meat, there is a diet called Pegan. It is a combo of Paleo and Vegan. It has some meat, but most of your diet is fruits, veggies, and nuts.

I won't even bring up the other diets. We have all known the list of diets over the decades. None of them last or have lasting success except the low meat, high vegetable, and healthy carb lifestyles. The blue zone way of eating is the healthiest. If someone asks if there is proof or science behind it, I'd say that centuries of small cultures eat in this way, being free of disease and sickness, free of pills, and living up to and beyond the hundred-year mark seems convincing. Yes? There are a few mini-series documentaries on Netflix: *Live to 100: Secrets of the Blue Zones* and *You Are What You Eat*.

Now, I've been vegan or plant-based on and off for years. I've always been this way in my heart, but I come from a history of a Midwestern diet. We ate pot roast and roasted whole chicken, beef, and pork sausage in our spaghetti sauce. I loved the taste of meat. I loved the smell of BBQ in the Summer, melted cheese, cheese and crackers, and poached eggs on toast. Because of this, I would go back to eating meat with much guilt. I had seen all the traumatic documentaries on factory farming, and I knew the cruelty. I justified it by buying the free-range and grass-fed; then, I learned that it didn't mean a thing. The chickens were still in warehouses but with just a few feet more to suffer in filth and overcrowding and never saw the sun. Grass-fed just meant a bit of grazing in the last few days. You need pasture-raised, and you need to learn all the trick labels that make it seem like compassionate farming is happening, but it's not. And if you do buy the local farm, compassionate, pasture-raised meat and eggs, it costs a fortune. Milk can be semi-compassionate, but it's not. Constantly impregnating a cow and then taking her baby away at birth is not compassionate. Sticking a baby calf in a small igloo or stall to be fattened for veal is not compassionate, no matter how we try to make it ok in our minds.

But cheese and meat are addictive. They are also getting more expensive and scarier to eat. Cases of E. coli and salmonella are becoming common on the store shelves. Parasites are also common in stored meat. Antibiotics are fed throughout the raising process because the chickens, beef, or pigs are raised in such filthy, crowded conditions that they are always sick. Hence, they get a constant drip of antibiotics in the meat. People are now becoming antibiotic-resistant more than ever. Let's skip the part about all the diseases that started from factory-farmed meat and chicken farms. More will come, so it feels like Russian roulette whenever I cook a meat dish.

I go back and forth with meat, but a few years back, I was vegan for a whole year. I had so much fun in the kitchen; it was the most creative scratch cooking ever. I veganized everything! I made vegan burgers, shakes, casseroles, lasagna, pizzas, stir-fries, cakes, frostings, enchiladas, lentil loaf, sloppy joes, and mushroom stroganoffs. I loved watching vegan cooking videos and finding vegan cookbooks at the library. It gave me a whole new zest for cooking. Then I went back to meat. Within six months, I returned to a more plant-based diet, meaning it's less political and intense. I sometimes eat honey and have some old Ugg boots I'm not throwing out. I have wavered back and forth since. My family still wants meat, eggs, and dairy. I get tired of cooking for me. However, each time, I was a little more uncomfortable with it, and I found myself getting more disturbed when preparing meat, especially whole chicken or turkey bodies. I felt a little repulsed at the cold flesh, and often, I found bruises on the bodies, which made it more disturbing. I never was into eggs after having our factory farm rescue chickens. After seeing how sick these birds were and how their beaks had been cut off so they wouldn't kill each other in such confined spaces where they go mad, I just wasn't into eating eggs anymore. I also noticed that when I went back to drinking dairy, even pasture-raised, I felt soreness in my joints, especially my fingers.

When I eat plant-based, I feel the best, look the best, and feel clean inside and out. My breath isn't bad, my underarms don't stink after a while, and my body odor stays reasonably clean. Carnivores attest to feeling the same, but it's because, at first, they have removed all the processed foods, junk foods, and sugar. That makes them feel good, but I'm afraid I have to disagree that they don't smell bad. Most hard-core meat eaters have a smell. My chiropractor eats high amounts of meat, and I smell it on his breath. He says vegetables are not natural for us to digest, and he talks about feeling great being in ketosis for years. That just can't be good for our bodies. You starve your body of carbs that it needs for the brain, cells, and muscles, so it begins eating your muscles. He is slim but doesn't have clear, white eyes or glowing skin. Most high meat eaters have this look; they don't have the shine and glow or sparkle of the eye. It's a touchy subject, though. I never say a word because people love their meat and will defend it with their lives. Sort of how I feel about coffee.

I have a vegan neighbor. She started eating meat again in the last year or so. She and I were chatting about it one day, and she said her friend told her she looked so much better now that she was eating meat, but she exclaimed, "I gained 40 pounds, and I don't look or feel better at all". Why do meat eaters do this? They act like we are killing ourselves without it and act so relieved when we start eating again. The truth is that we are killing ourselves by eating the average American way. When we go plant-based, we are returning to health and balance. Why are meat eaters advocating this diet like anything else is sure death? To each his own. Do what makes you feel good. But try and be aware of the toll it takes on animals and the environment. Get blood work done.

The only time a vegan or plant-based diet becomes unhealthy is when people with eating disorders start cutting out this and that and getting weird about it. They cut out oil, nuts, and salt and get so strict. A healthy diet must have a lot of variety and balance. You don't have to do plant-based or vegan perfectly. Just cutting down on your meat and dairy intake and maybe raising your own eggs or buying from local farms makes a huge difference. You support small farmers who care a bit more, and animals have a better life.

Last year, I was downsizing the furniture again and giving away a substantial King-sized foam mattress and box springs. It was so big it took up the whole bedroom. I was getting a smaller bed for free. A woman came to pick up the mattress and box springs and brought two men to help her. I was so taken with these men. It wasn't that they were handsome. They were older, maybe in their late sixties, but they were so fit and glowing with this fantastic health that I stared at them. They wore cargo pants and nice fitting shirts that looked like natural cotton and natural colors, not old, stained, baggy shirts or baggy jeans with holes. They were dressed in clothes that were neutral, clean, and well-fitting. Their bodies were very trim and fit, not buff or unnatural, just lean and toned. Their skin glowed. It was clear and had a slight tan, radiating this healthy glow. Their eyes sparkled, and the whites were very white. Their hair was natural silver and shiny. You can tell what a person eats and invibes by the texture of their hair, the color and texture of their skin, and the whites of their eyes. And, of course, their bodies. We show in our bodies what we put in them.

I had some ideas about this year. I wanted to eat more vegetables and exercise a little more. And get rid of the sugar. That was about it. I didn't think I would try to go raw, which doesn't work 100%; I don't even think I knew I'd go back to plant-based and commit. But now, here I am. I'm plant-based and doing it as clean and homemade as possible, even cleaning out my pantry of Crisco and sugar. I eat a lot of raw; I'll be 70 to 80% raw when the seasons get warm. Who wants a cold salad in rainy weather? Ah, but when it's hot out, all I want are fresh, crisp salads, and I can't wait for the melon season!

I've been doing a parasite cleans and a liver detox. This is after I had done a couple of rounds of Mastic Gum and Slippery Elm. These will be the only cleanses I'll do. People can get nutty about cleansing repeatedly and forever. We eat a lot of produce, more than most, but we got into this habit of having snacks and sweets in the house all the time. We have years of eating meat and dairy. I have a history of extreme diets and junk food, and fast food. I was raised on formula and secondhand smoke and had years of drinking and smoking myself. A good, deep clean will help heal the past.

The only way to get shiny hair, clear eyes, a fit body, and glowing skin is to eat a clean diet filled with fruits and vegetables and keep all the processed foods and sugar out, not to take pills or alcohol, cigarettes, or any drug. It's tough to change these addictions, but once they are gone and a few months to a year have passed, it changes your life. I know from experience. I never liked drugs or pills, but I did drink and smoke cigarettes and pot for over two decades. It took me a year of completely changing my lifestyle to overcome these habits and addictions. It's been fourteen years since I quit everything, and I don't miss it one bit.

I struggled for years to quit my bad habits. I'll tell you how I finally healed myself and quit all my habits. But first, let's look at why it's so important to quit.

Smoking alone is very expensive. I think a pack of cigarettes costs almost $10, and if you are a pack-a-day smoker, that is $300 a month. Beer, wine, and hard liquor can run hundreds of dollars a month, even if it's only on the weekends or a bottle of wine at dinner. Drugs, well, I have no idea what people are doing now for drugs or the cost, but the cost in life and spirit is enough.

The most significant cost is the cost to our health. Our mental health and balance, our physical health. If we have habits or addictions, they may seem to be our personal choice, but they aren't. They affect our children, our families, and our community. When a partner smokes for a lifetime, their health declines and the family has to take care of them when they get emphysema or as they decline with lung cancer. My mother was a smoker and drinker, and I had to leave my life many times to come home and take care of her. She had lung cancer, where they were able to remove parts of her lung, and then for the remaining years, she suffered emphysema, and that is a horrible way to live. You feel like you're suffocating all the time.

Drinking and drugs deteriorate our minds and pollute our bodies. A person ages quickly and becomes someone else mentally and emotionally. Often, someone unpleasant to be around.

At the very least, people lose a lot of money and stay severely broke because of these habits or addictions. This goes for gambling and shopping addictions. Those are detrimental to our wallet and our mental well-being and affect our families. Spending money on our habits instead of taking our kids on trips and doing fun things with them is a sad problem.

The only way to overcome an addiction is to get help, a support group, and change your lifestyle. Depending on the addiction, the changes go from a few changes to an extreme lifestyle makeover. When I changed my life and let go of all my habits, I moved to a new town on the coast and joined AA. I went to all the meetings, did everything they told me to do, and made new friends. I showed up to meetings early and set up chairs; I stayed after and washed cups, attended daily, went to every social event, listened to other people's stories, and shared myself when I had some time under my belt. My old friends didn't invite me around much anymore because it's uncomfortable having a sober person around when you're drinking and smoking, and this worked out well because I couldn't hang out with old friends doing old habits. I had new friends who were also living a clean and healthy lifestyle. I went to sober parties; I had potlucks with my new friends. I even listened to new music, watched new movies, and visited new places. Old music and places and people can be strong triggers, and when you are building a new life, it's like a tender little garden start; it needs to be protected from the elements until it's big and strong. I lived in a safe bubble for a solid year, and my whole life changed. After all that hard work, I built a fantastic life. I married and became a mother and went on to become a writer and an influencer for years. We bought two houses and have lived very well.

This goes for how we feed ourselves and care for our bodies. We get addicted to junk food, sugar, dairy, meat, and sodas. We become sedentary. We overfeed ourselves and our families. Premade food is a luxury when we are too tired to cook, but it is filled with chemicals and dyes, extra oils and sugars, and less-than-quality ingredients. It's okay for a few occasions but not for a daily meal. The foods the average American is consuming are making them sick with diabetes, obesity, high cholesterol, and high blood pressure. Even the "healthy" diets for weight loss are doing damage and rarely are successful. It's hard to break the cycle and embrace a healthy way of eating and living.

Recently, I was moved to change our diet and lifestyle because I noticed we were all getting or staying a bit overweight. I could lose a good 50 lbs. myself.

I had to purge my pantry, chest freezer, fridge, cupboards, and little freezer. I had a lot of healthy foods, so we were set, but each time I grocery shop, I only buy the clean, essential foods: produce, whole grains and beans, plant milk, nuts, and seasonings. When I use the food bank, I request only the produce, rice, beans, and plant milks and I have us listed as vegetarians. I don't take the sweets and treats they offer, mac and cheese, meats, dairy, and rarely the eggs. If we get peanut butter, I use it for cookies for school events or for our librarians. The peanut butter they give us is the junky kind with sugar and oil. We buy clean peanut butter with nothing but peanuts. You can make your own, too.

We cut way back on the TV time, listening to music most of the day. There is no gaming, YouTube, and limited internet for study. We still have movies and TV series. We go out to parks and trails, ride bikes, and spend sunny days outside on the porch reading, strolling through the neighborhood, or being busy with the house and garden. This has had such great results on our moods and health. It's not easy to change all this with a family. The kids may fight the changes, especially if you are taking away gaming, the internet, and YouTube. It's all made to be highly addictive. But once they detox, the personality change is worth it. Personally, I feel my kids are too young to start all this gaming obsession. YouTube and the internet have good things but also a lot of junk I don't have time to sit and keep an eye on to filter out for them. I felt it was influencing them too much and negatively. They would disagree and weren't happy about me shutting it down, but I see their personalities blossoming again; they are calmer and are not learning all this negative junk online.

Only you know what is best for you and your family. We are saving a lot of money, and our mental, physical, and spiritual health is thriving. I will say that our physical and mental health is the most important thing. When it is compromised or deteriorated, we struggle, live in depression, and become broke in spirit or financially. It's not a good life.

Anything that affects our mental health must be seriously looked at and eliminated or altered. Negative relationships, jobs that suck the life out of us, too much online life, and social media. Maybe we must eliminate a friend, distance ourselves from in-laws, or quit a job. Your happiness and sanity is worth it.

We live on a small income but feel middle class, and we are very happy and content. I have let go of relationships, schedules, foods, and all kinds of things that were compromising our utmost health and vibrancy. It took years and plenty of trial and error. It is worth it in the end.

Chapter Four

A Happy Mind Is Free And Invaluable

I'm not against therapy. Talking is great. But sometimes, a good therapist is expensive, and what if you don't have money? Getting a therapist is painful, and when I tried to get a therapist toward the end of the quarantine, I was either never called back or forgotten after a call or two. I decided to take matters into my own hands. I found a way to do therapy free and in my way. I could tailor it to my liking. I would not suggest this for everyone, but I've had some experience, and I'm sober and learned a few tricks with The Center For Spiritual Living. I've had healers and clairvoyants work with me, and I've had some training in meditation and treatment prayers.

Since moving up to the mountains, I was introduced to the Tibetan Monks, who visit this town yearly. The monks gather for a few weeks in a small hall in the countryside and a few miles from our home. They teach, bless animal shelters, and have ceremonies and group healing. I attend every healing every year. This is my third year. The group healings involve chanting, visualization, and rituals, and then we are given a string to wear that the Dalai Lama blesses.

I have done these healings and transformed. Was it a placebo effect from believing the healings work magic, or does the energy of the healing and the energy of the monks seep into our soul and help us elevate to a higher state of being?

I'm not inspired to sit and meditate for long periods, but I enjoy playing a game where I try to keep my mind clear while doing daily tasks or taking walks with Molly. I notice how she stops, sniffs the air, perks up her little ears, and looks deep into the woods. I doubt she's thinking anything. She is feeling and hearing, smelling and sensing. I try to mimic her. I quiet my mind and hear the wind and birds, the rustling of leaves, and the distant sounds of the town. I struggle to keep my mind quiet and peaceful, but if I keep practicing, eventually, I piece together some moments of silence in my mind. We all lack a quiet mind with all the noise of life and social media, the news, YouTube, and traffic. Our brains are exhausted with overstimulation and too much information. We come from ancestors who lived by the seasons and quietly went through the forest to hunt or gather berries and herbs. We had to be quiet to survive. Now, we have no quiet, and our dopamine has spiked so often that it's depleted. We are mentally drained and depressed.

The fix for that is to turn off the news and computer vices and go back to quietly going about our day or maybe having a little music in the background.

I've had the White Dzambhala Empowerment healing recently. It is about removing the incorrect thinking of poverty consciousness, lack, and fear and bringing abundance to stay focused on our Dharma. Dharma has many meanings, but it is mostly our spiritual path. I loved this healing because it helped me lose my fears of insufficient money and the pressure to produce and hustle to pay the bills. This is wonderful because now, with the pressure to constantly hustle and make money eliminated, I have faith that the Universe will provide, and I can focus on my inner work. Less focus on money and worldly things and more turning inward to find peace and prosperity.

After this significant healing, there were three more. I attended every one of them, sitting through hours of chanting and visualizing, choking on incense and devouring every minute with absolute focus. I know how powerful they are.

I decided that after the healings, I would stay offline. I do have email to check, and sometimes, the bank or book sales; I minimize my time on YouTube, which I can get sucked into. I stay off blogs and have never enjoyed social media. It's hard. I reach for the phone now and then and have this urge to scroll and get on YouTube and find videos on this and that. However, the truth is that I have books for every interest, and I can turn to them for gardening, vegan cooking, spiritual work, or entertainment. I'm a 70s child and remember what we did and how we learned before the internet and cell phones. We read.

Years ago, when the children were babies, I had no interest in the internet. I played music or silence all day, read novels, and read children's books to the littles all day.

I remember life being more peaceful and I was far more content and fulfilled when the internet was a laptop on a desk in the corner gathering dust. Our TV reception was from an antenna on the roof, and we only received PBS, a classic movie channel, and some black and white westerns. I spent my days reading, freshening the house, cooking, and focusing on my children. That was it. I wasn't hustling, writing, filming, blogging, and on the internet all the time. I had one priority: family. Home goes with that. We need a clean, cozy home, healthy, delicious meals, and daily rituals to raise a happy family. I remember that time with great fondness.

I began to lose that calm contentment and slow pace of life when I started a writing career, then a blog, *and* then a YouTube channel. When we bought our first house, we worked on it a lot initially, but it was small with small gardens, so it was fun and doable. We have been working hard for almost four years with Arthur, our current home.

After spending a year working on the electricity, plumbing, gutting, and redoing the second bathroom, and rebuilding the foundation by hand, I begged Bali that we would not do any more DIY projects. I want to go back to a simple existence. Just sweep the floors and plant some seeds in the garden. I can't take all this laborious work every day.

Recently, my two old dogs passed. They have left an empty space, and the yard is now quiet. That makes me sad from time to time. I still have my little Molly, and she's young and adorable, so I have a doggie dolly to play with and fuss over. However, I will be honest, I feel some relief, and life is a bit easier. Tending to two old dogs is hospice care for a pet instead of a human. They needed to be watched over, and I made a lot of homemade dog food and bone broth when they seemed to have stomach issues or their teeth were getting sensitive. There were accidents in the house that required scrubbing. They needed expensive dental appointments. There were sleepless nights when one dog suffered Sundowners syndrome, that is, when an old dog has dementia, and it kicks in at night. They become nervous, paced, and pant all night. I found hemp oil fixed this problem. Then, the other dog suffered arthritis, and hemp oil only helped so much. Having three dogs was a bit much for me. Now that I have one small dog, the experience is so different. It's easy and playful. Having this little dog is like having another baby but without the complete work of a human baby. She has her routines and toys, her baths and walks. I'm having so much fun with her these days. I never stress about returning home for the other dogs or exercising three dogs daily. Most of Molly's food is homemade now, and one big pot will last for weeks instead of just a week. The yard is immaculate now. It's much easier now and more enjoyable.

I don't watch the news or read things online. I find that I run across articles that upset me, and if it's about children or animals, I can be upset and disturbed for weeks. Remember that most articles and news clips are exaggerated and sensationalized to get views and ratings. Remember that the news focuses only on the negative. The only news worth reading is good news. There are lovely good news outlets. I used to love Positive News. You can get the magazine or browse online for free. I want to know what is going right in the world, and that inspires me to help increase the good.

When I watched the news, I felt it was all terrible; what was the use of going on? And that is why many suicides happen. There is no hope. There was a Native

American Chief who said that taking away a man's hope is a cruel thing. He said it more wisely, but that was the gist of it. Taking away a person's hope is cruel; you leave them empty and fill the space with fear. Fear harms the spirit and can make people mean and start wars. Hope brings a spring to our step and helps us look forward to each new day.

Many spiritual teachings tell us to go into the wilderness to heal. Lao Tzu, who wrote the Tao Te Ching, saw the violence and corruption of his times, so he packed up his ox and went into the wilderness to live in peace. The Bible says not to be of the world. Buddha said, "With our thoughts, we make the world." Buddha said, "Health is the greatest gift, contentment the greatest wealth, faithfulness the best relationship."

We removed the internet for over a year, maybe two years, and it was the best decision. We spent every weekend at the library and got to know all the librarians, brought them platters of cookies, and picked their brilliant minds for ideas on books, movies, and games. I still drop the kids off one day a week to play for a few hours, and I love to chat with my favorites. They know us by name and help me get any book or movie I desire. They used to ensure we had a Hot Spot before every holiday and let us keep it a little longer than the return date. I idolize the librarians and the Tibetan Monks.

Back then, we watched movies and didn't always have the outside world invading our space. We have internet in our house again for school, and I've had to set many boundaries. But I remember what it was like, and I always go back to that 1970s-style of living. I prefer to have music playing in the house all the time. Sometimes, I may put on a movie and have that on in the background. I'm one of those silly people who has to have some noise and energy in the house. I'm not good with dead silence, as much as that would benefit my mind.

The more time I spend in my sanctuary, surrounded by all that is kind and lovely, beautiful, colorful, and lush, the more I'm aware of how negative things, be they the news or grumpy people, affect me. I have a sensitive heart and can't take it all in.

For me, the Tibetan Monks are worth years of the best therapy out there. I have gone every year and had two group healings each time. This was my third year, and I did all three offered healings. They were long and deep, and I was worn out after each one. I felt different after all of them and had to sleep a lot. I've had to keep to myself because I'm like an open vessel, and I feel everyone's energy around me. I had to leave Raley's the other day mid-shopping because it was so crowded, and I felt overwhelmed by all the people and their energies. Sadly, so many people are unhappy, stressed, unhealthy in body and mind, suffering addictions and miseries. I have been there, and you try everything to be better and look better and feel better, but it is a hard fight to overcome our habits or addictions. Many things we think are addictions are only deeply rooted habits. However, to pull those roots out is work. I discussed this in another chapter, but to change a habit or addiction, you need to change everything. Albert Einstein said, "We cannot solve problems at the same level of thinking we were when we created those problems."

If you want to overcome an addiction and have a happy, healthy life, you must recreate your whole life. I talked about this in the previous chapter.

It's straightforward to heal the body and mind. Get rid of the junk. Both online junk and food junk are being sold to us. Everything is being made to be very addictive on purpose, so we will keep coming back, and we will keep buying the products. They make stuff cheap, so we buy, buy, buy. They sensationalize news, so we can't help but click on it. The food industry, the diet industry, the pharmaceutical industry, the news industry, the big box stores…they are all getting rich. Meanwhile, we are getting bigger, sadder, and sicker. And poorer with debt. It's time to wake up.

News is not allowed at all, ever. This doesn't mean I'm checked out. I sign petitions and donate small amounts to this cause and that cause. We vaguely know what is happening, but the best way to help is to live well and show our life as an example. We can volunteer, support good organizations, and put our money into good things. We can choose not to put money or energy into negative things.

I've been reading a lot of Dolores Cannon's books lately. You need an open mind for what is taught in her books, but I find the books exciting and hopeful. I read *The Keepers Of The Garden, The Search For Hidden, Sacred Knowledge,* and *The Three Waves Of Volunteers And The New Earth.* I seek spiritual information about our Universe and ourselves, and I immensely love my spiritual life. It has given me such faith and peace. It is not traditional, and it is not religious in any way. There is no sin or end of times in my beliefs. My beliefs go on to infinity in the possibilities.

Chapter Five

Old Cars Or On Foot

We have a Toyota Corolla and a Toyota Tacoma truck. Both get excellent gas mileage, even that old truck. I can get to Oregon from California on one tank of gas. Both vehicles are close to 300,000 miles and counting. We have taken good care of them, including oil changes and tune-ups, updated brakes, coils, tires, and filters. We live in a small town, and everything is within walking distance. We can even walk to the next small town over the hill. We walk a lot. We walk to the small Safeway downtown when we need a few items and to various trails on either side of our neighborhood. In the Summer, we walk to the food bank to volunteer one day a week.

We don't travel much. We may visit our close friends in Oregon every couple of years. We used to visit friends in the Bay Area and family in Tahoe, but everyone is busy, and we seem to stay within a few miles of home these days. Our cars are paid for, and we have cheap car insurance. We use them sparingly.

The car has a cracked windshield, and the truck's windshield has a starter crack. The paint is peeling on both modes of transportation. The truck has a few dents on the sides from me getting in and out of the driveway. The fence is always in the way. I recently removed the passenger side mirror due to the gate swinging in the way as I pulled out. I also don't know why they put the telephone pole near our driveway. It's pretty much in our driveway! And who needs a telephone pole anymore? So, that has gotten in the way as well.

Our vehicles aren't pretty, but do I care? No! My car takes me everywhere without giving me trouble. I never get in that car and worry I won't return home. That truck has moved us two times from town to town...no, it's moved us three times! It has hauled sand, gravel, horse manure, and free stuff I find on the street or Craigslist.

Having solid, paid-for cars is a gift and not a burden. I think most of us could live with one car just fine, but it would require us to stop running around all the time and spend more time at home. Not everyone likes to be at home. We are fortunate to have so many things to walk to. City dwellers and Europeans understand this. They take public transportation for everything or walk everywhere. Only in America did we start zoning and building towns spread out with suburbs far away from town and towns with ten-lane roads. This was on purpose, so we had to have cars to get around. This serves the car companies and the oil companies. However, I see this changing as gas prices change and people want more walkable cities and towns. Walkable towns are more attractive, and people are more fit and connected to their community. You can't connect with your environment if you are always in a car zooming about.

Let's take back our roads and health and get out there with bikes, skateboards, even roller skates!

Chapter Six

Our Humble But Luxurious Life

I love the mornings, especially in the winter, when I bustle about opening curtains and turning things on. With a click, push, or turn of buttons and knobs, the house begins to fill with light, warmth, music, and the smell of fresh brewing coffee. That feels like wealth right there. We have warmth, and I have hot, fresh, creamy coffee—a big mug. Music makes life like a good movie with theme music.

I have so many things I want to do, and I want to read and learn each day. I have dishes I want to try in the kitchen. I often hurry back to my computer to write down ideas of characters and stories I might forget if I don't type them out right then and there. My days feel like a dance between chores and writing, and I love it.

I have rituals, too. This morning, I had a long talk with Oregon (my friend in Oregon), and I read her a chapter from my latest Dolores Cannon book, *The Three Waves Of Volunteers.* She and I love exploring spirituality and healing naturally for our bodies and minds; we talk about aliens and a new future; she reads my astral chart often, and we love metaphysics and our guides. Each friend I have, we talk about different topics at different levels. I enjoy my chats with coffee so very much. I look forward to a morning chat that can sometimes span into a two-hour conversation.

I work out every day. Sometimes, I work out in the morning and later take a long walk with Molly, and a child or two might join us now and then. I do an easy half hour with the elliptical and then some arms and legs on our Marcy Home Gym. I notice how much stronger I am sometimes when doing household tasks. Moving furniture is light work; even whipping a stiff batter is easier now. I feel so strong when I walk or deep clean the house. I don't have the aches and pains. More than the desire to lose weight, this motivates me, and I look forward to my morning workouts. We have a whole gym in our house. All the pieces are small, so it doesn't seem obnoxious. The pieces blend in each room. A stationary bike in the living room, elliptical in my office and the Marcy Home Gym in the bedroom corner.

I have to be honest; I'm not loving the bike. It makes my nether regions numb. But everyone else loves working out on the bike while watching TV. I have ankle weights to wear as I walk about and small weights to do in-between. I have a few favorite yoga videos on YouTube. A free and cozy gym, and I don't have to leave the house. I used to love joining clubs, working out, swimming, and going to the sauna. Health clubs are great, and maybe one day down the road I'll join one again, but right now, I'm too lazy to drive there and back, and I have this home that is hard to leave. All the equipment was inexpensive or free.

I have customized this home, and even the boys don't want to leave because it's so cozy and offers us so many good things. We like to go for a short time and rush back. We have all our delights here.

My cookbooks and my homemaking books are an immense delight. I love my books. I do love cooking videos because I learn better by watching and doing. But I love my physical cookbooks and browsing through them at a sunny table and making lists of things to bake and cook in bulk or new dishes, candy, and loaves of bread to try. Most of my cooking has been from **Cheap And Good** by LeAnne Brown. She wrote it for people on food stamps. It's easy, scratch cooking, and we've enjoyed a few of her recipes. I've made many dishes from Simply Sara Kitchen on YouTube. I like her old videos and her vegetarian or vegan dishes. I have her recipes written down and do the minestrone and mushroom stroganoff often. I used to love **Dump Dinners** by Cathy Mitchel. I just changed the recipes with plant-based milk, butter, faux meats, and cheeses. You can veganize anything, and I have more fun transforming regular recipes into healthier and vegan ones.

I enjoy a clean house; it gives me peace of mind, and I'm more productive in a clean, tidy house. It's a bit funky and bohemian, with warmth and charm. I have a huge front porch with a hammock and wicker chairs so we can read and drink iced tea when the weather is warm. Sam loves making giant Sun tea in jars, which we buy for a couple of dollars at WinCo. I think we still have a package for this Summer. BBQing is another thing we love to do. And swim. We have a pool, and there is just something about having a pool in the Summer. The smell of BBQ and chlorine fills me with Summertime nostalgia.

I have such a great time playing with my home. I love decorating, purging, organizing, freshening, tidying, rearranging, and beautifying. I loved my dollhouses as a little girl, and now I have a home to enjoy and feel happy and safe. It's good to feel grateful for a home. It may not be beautiful, but it's amazing what paint and plants can do to a house. A swept porch and garden in the yard will make your home very sweet, even if the paint is peeling.

I look forward to each season and what it brings: Summer is swimming, library days, so much fresh fruit and vegetables, and BBQ. Winter is filled with holidays. Fall is Halloween and cool weather, changing of the leaves and the smell of wood smoke in the crisp air. Spring is gorgeous and lush, and time to put in the garden. I enjoy each one.

I enjoy the morning rituals, the afternoons in the kitchen making supper, and the evening TV time. I enjoy my bubble baths and when I have books waiting for me at the library. I love the time when I prepare to sit down and write. I put on my little espresso pot to make another mug of steaming Joe and settle in front of the laptop. There are so many joys in each day, throughout the day and in each year, each season, each holiday or solstice, or whatever you prefer. I feel like I have something to look forward to all the time.

Chapter Seven

A Scratch Kitchen

We did a trip to WinCo the other day. WinCo is in a couple of towns in either direction of us, but each town is at least 30 minutes away. I visit WinCo every four months when I have my dentist appointment in the valley. I like combining these because they are in the same town. Saves on gas and trips out of town. I used to spend at least $400 to $600 each time, but I would stock up the pantry for a few months. I bought healthy things, boxed things, canned things. No meat or eggs because they scare me there. It's pretty much all factory-farmed stuff. But I would buy cereal, canned beans, sauces, and boxed stuffing. I'd buy cheese and butter.

This visit the other day was the first time going to WinCo since switching to plant-based and scratch-cooking everything. Lately, I find store-bought sauces and premade foods to taste weird. The sauces have a bitter aftertaste, and processed foods are bland or bitter. It works to make everything myself, but it's also satisfying and fun. I have so many scratch-and-mix cookbooks. I have **Make A Mix** books and ***Make Your Groceries, More Make Your Groceries, Dump Dinners, Fix It And Forget It, The New Farm Vegetarian Cookbook, Good And Cheap, Make Your Mixes And Prepared Foods***, and many more homemade cooking books. I love them. I think I'm a little addicted to them. I love finding used copies and then waiting eagerly by the mailbox for their arrival into my life. I then spend all evening pouring over them.

With the **Make A Mix** books, you can make huge batches of homemade pancake mixes, Bisquick-type mixes, and even sauces and meat dishes you can freeze. You can do a lot of batch cooking and make mixes over the weekend and be set for months. This is perfect for working folks. It will save so much money, and you have clean, healthy foods without the chemicals, dyes, preservatives, and extra sugars. You'll make your own boxed, premade, frozen meals and mixes.

I love YouTube videos about vegan or plant-based cooking. A new channel for me is **Simnett Nutrition**. He is a fantastic cook, and the dishes are very healthy. He makes replicas of delicious vegan mock products such as queso nacho sauce from Costco and the Just Eggs faux egg stuff that costs something crazy, like $8 for a small bottle. He makes it out of natural ingredients and for pennies. **Thee Burger Dude** is another vegan channel. Some other channels that teach cooking from scratch are **HealthyVeganEating, Turnip Vegan, My Vegan Kitchen Life, We Cook Vegan, Derek Sarno, and PB with J.**

If you don't have the money to collect used books from Thriftbooks or Amazon, you can get so many at the library and watch cooking vlogs on YouTube. You don't have to buy a single book. I just ordered (library) **The Complete Plant-Based Cookbook by America's Test Kitchen**. It has 500 recipes. I can't wait to look it over. I have a notebook that I copy recipes in from these books because we are on a no "extra" period.

Vegan eating can be delicious and extremely healthy. Vegan cooking is the most fun I have ever had in the kitchen. It breathed new life into my kitchen life.

It is also the cheapest and most accessible on my grocery budget. If I were to buy all the processed and premade vegan meats and mixes, granolas, and cookies, my bill would be high, but I make it all at home with simple ingredients. It might be less healthy if I bought the premade, but I make meats and cheeses with lentils, root vegetables, and spices.

After playing around with recipes on and off for years, I have realized that most recipes have the same base seasonings.

My vegan pantry has these items:

Paprika
Smoked paprika.
Onion powder, granulated, and flakes.
Garlic powder, granulated.
Vegetable bouillon
Gluten
Ketchup
Mustard (Dijon is great)
Basil

Sage
Italian seasoning
Mustard powder
Thyme
Rosemary
Flax seeds
Nutritional yeast
Raw cashews
Dates
BarBQ sauce
Sriracha
Vegan Worcestershire sauce
Yeast
Olive oil
Baking soda
Corn starch
Baking Powder
Soy sauce
Salt
Pepper

Then we have the main food staples:
Oats
All Purpose flour (have it be 10% protein or higher to make gluten)
Wheat flour (I buy pastry; it's cheapest and works fine)
Pinto beans are the cheapest
Brown rice is the cheapest
White rice, if you have a preference
Lentils (red and brown are needed for various recipes)
Yellow split mung beans (to make Just Eggs)
Garbanzos
Soybeans
Tons of produce: fruits and vegetables, lemons, limes, berries
Tofu
Almonds
Walnuts
Cashews

Canned and Frozen produce
Onions, Garlic, Peppers
Potatoes of all kinds
Squash of all kinds

With this simple pantry, you can make everything! There is no need to buy crackers, pizza dough, tortillas, pancakes, cakes, cookies, breads, muffins, and biscuits. You can make them from the pantry ingredients. You can make faux chicken, steak, baloney, vegan cheese sauces, and vegan cheeses. You can also make plant milk, plant butter, and plant eggs.

I don't buy specialty seasonings or ingredients unless it's for a recipe I know we love and will make often. I buy groceries and seasonings to make repetitive dishes, such as flour. I buy 50 lbs. of flour because I make so many things from that flour. I make gluten from All Purpose flour alone to make gluten steaks and shredded barbequed chicken; you can even make sweet and sour pork. You can make every bread and cake item you can imagine. From tofu, I make scrambles, grilled barbequed sandwiches, and mozzarella cheese. With nutritional yeast and cashews, I can make cheese sauces and many other vegan dishes and sauces.

You don't need to buy spaghetti sauce. Just sauté tomatoes in olive oil with garlic and basic and then blend. That is also great for pizzas. When tomatoes are in season, or you grow your own, the sauce is out of this world. I canned many quarts of spaghetti sauce this year from just a few tomato plants. Tomato plants can start small and humble but grow into huge, tall bushes, especially if you prune them well.

It took three years of amending our once gravel and weed yard, but it now produces well. Last year, I sauteed bell peppers and onions for burritos and yellow zucchini in butter. Then we had eggplant and potato Indian dishes, all the canned spaghetti sauce, and some cans of tomatoes and basil—all from the garden. Our fruit trees produced a few breakfasts and snacks, and I collected half a gallon of raw almonds.

Growing organic food is fun. I say fun because when the garden and trees begin to produce for the first time, it is a thrilling thing. Walking out in your garden every morning, harvesting a basket of live, fresh produce, and creating a menu for the day around the feast is a creative, inspiring moment. The flavors are like nothing you will get in a store, not even in a health food store, because the fruits and vegetables are picked and cooked within hours or minutes. And you save a fortune. We can eat hundreds of dollars of produce.

The only two places where I do my extensive grocery shopping are at the Grocery Outlet here in town, and every four months, I do a haul at WinCo out of town. I used to buy many groceries, but now I don't need much. At Grocery Outlet, I stock up on frozen, organic vegetables and fruit, fresh organic vegetables and fruit, whole grain sliced bread for lunch sandwiches because no one likes my homemade bread for sandwiches, and plant-based milk or creamers. If I find Date Syrup, I'll stock up on that, and sometimes I'll buy a few vegan meats or cheeses. Recently, we did a price comparison, and Bali says buying organic produce from the health food store is the same or cheaper, so we have three stores now.

Here is what I bought on the last trip to WinCo (and this will last for two to three months):

25 lbs. White Popcorn
5 lbs. Nutritional Yeast
5 lbs. Gluten
3 lbs. Yeast (for baking and pizza dough)
10 lbs. Raw Cashew pieces
1 lb. Garlic powder
½ lb. Turmeric
½ lb. Curry powder
12 cans of black olives (for pizzas)
5 lbs. Coconut pieces (they are sweetened, and I eat them as a treat)
9 lbs. Spaghetti pasta
5 lbs. Raw Pumpkin seeds
3 lbs. Organic Yellow Potatoes (this is the only produce from there; the rest didn't look great at this store, and I get my produce from Grocery Outlet)
10 24 oz. cans of Hunts Traditional Pasta Sauce (used to be .99 cents, now $1.42, but still cheaper than jars of spaghetti sauce)
2 10 lb. bags of King Arthurs Unbleached All-Purpose Flour 11.7% Gluten forming protein content

It came to $184.00.

These items help round out my pantry and are essential to making homemade vegan foods and substitutes.

We volunteer at the food pantry and are also members of this food pantry. I love the food bank. We make a small living, have a tight budget, and don't have food stamps. Maybe we qualify now as I'm not bringing in the extra money from my channel, but the food bank is fantastic because much of the food is donated from local grocery stores and bakeries. It is food that would otherwise be thrown in dumpsters and added to the landfills. It is almost expired or hit the "best by" date. It is leftover produce from the fields and orchards. The food pantry does purchase some foods. We are repurposing food that would otherwise be thrown away, and since we volunteer in the Summer, we somewhat earn it.

Some people think that the food pantry/bank is only for people down and out and with barren cupboards. I can tell you, from experience, that you better have somewhat of a pantry because the amount they give a family is only enough to make a few meals, last a few days, and some filler items. Since it's food from stores near expiration, it is random stuff. You may get a bag of raisins or canned pork, rice, and tomatoes ready to go South. You must learn to work with what you get. When I bring home the food bank allotments, I freeze the produce about to go bad or cook it up in a minestrone that day. Fruit that doesn't look too good is frozen for cakes and smoothies. I use old raisins in bread and cookies as they don't taste good just for eating plain; they are usually dried out too much. I use nuts in baking and making vegan dishes. The shelf stable and canned foods are good even past the 'best by' dates if the cans are not punctured.

I love getting home and unloading the boxes and bags to see what new and exciting items we will work with. I've discovered delicious vegan foods, sauces, and spice mixes that I never would have discovered. We keep our lentil, bean, and rice supplies up and always have enough produce for a few days. This helps tremendously, so when I have a hundred or a couple hundred dollars for groceries, I stock up as I showed, and these stock-ups last months. Especially if I go to the health food coop and order 50 lbs. of organic rice, beans, flour, and oats, these are often GMOs, so you want them organic, especially for plant-based people. I get 25 lbs. of organic Garbanzos now and then and steel-cut oats. These bags can last from two months to six months.

On average months, I rotate the food pantry every other week with a food bank that comes twice a month over the hill. It is a drive-through, and you get what you get. The exciting thing is that since going back to plant-based, I've been getting all sorts of wonderful vegan foods and only a lb. of ground beef. I cancel the milk when they are loading me up, and sometimes plant milk is in my box. I use ground beef to make a pot of dog food for Molly. I sauté it in a pot, add rice and canned vegetables from the food bank that we wouldn't usually use, and make a big soup pot of this homemade dog food that lasts her weeks. I freeze most of it.

With the other food pantry, we are listed as vegetarian, and I rarely take the eggs and ask for alternative milk instead of cows if they have it. So, I tailored it to make it vegan. I don't do the oats because they aren't non-GMO. I only do the rice and beans if we are running low. I say no to the sweets, treats, mac and cheese, but yes to extra produce and canned goods. We get soups and chili as a backup and sometimes canned tomatoes to make pizza sauce.

Sometimes, I get things we don't eat or don't eat often in my bags, but I put them to good use. I use the sugary peanut butter and eggs to make peanut butter cookies for Sam's class on special occasions like this Valentine's Day or the Librarian's when I drop the kids off for a day of gaming.
If I get extra meat, I give it to my neighbor who is also on a tight budget.

We always get vegan faux meats, tempeh, hot dogs, and Seitan in our vegetarian bags, so we've had to learn how to work with these things. We also get treats that I put in the kids' lunches.

I'll tell you, though, as we progress in our plant-eating, our grocery bill is getting smaller and smaller. I need the food banks to help less and less. If I stock up on 25 lb. and 50 lb. bags of rice, beans, oats, and flour, I don't need those from the food pantry. I don't need staples if I stock up on some canned items at WinCo. If I find deals on plant milk, I buy plenty and throw the extras in the chest freezer. We recently bought a box of organic vegetables at the health food store, and it was the same or cheaper than the Grocery Outlet. We bought a big, full box of produce for $34. That isn't bad.

Scratch cooking is easier than one would think. I suggest getting a **Make A Mix** book on Thriftbooks or Amazon. I got all my books used and cheap. If you have no money, download *LeAnne Brown's* **Cheap And Good.** Learn to shop once a month and spend a weekend bulk cooking and making mixes, and you will be set for a month or more. This would be perfect for single or double-working parents. You will save so much money, and the food will be much healthier. Buying organics isn't expensive if you buy basics in season, not premade and packaged. If you buy what I listed and make everything, your monthly bill will be smaller as you stock up on things.

Today was Sam's birthday. We had a small budget, and Sam chose the food we would put out as a spread on the table. At first, I was thrilled with this because I didn't have to cook at all. I usually bake cakes and cook birthday meals. I make the whole spread that goes on the table for the partygoers. This time, I could open, set up, and walk away. However, I was highly disappointed when I opened the plastic packages and looked over the trays, putting everything out on pretty serving platters. The food was of poor quality but expensive. We bought a vegetable tray with plenty of carrots but only half an old celery chopped in chunks, a few broccoli florets, half a handful of snap peas, and three peppers. Very little for $14.99. The charcuterie board had cornstarch-dusted cheese, salami, and crackers, which was not so bad for the price but lacking in freshness. The Stouffer's enchiladas barely fed five people and were very stingy with the sauce and cheese; it must have been an ounce or two on the whole pan. The prices are increasing, and the foods have less "food." The companies also use the cheapest factory-farmed meats, eggs, dairy, and fillers like GMO rice or wheat and skimp on the good stuff.

Then we have all the plastic packaging—lots of packaging. To summarize this party table tragedy, I could make an organic fruit spread, vegetable spread, cake, and large casserole that was deliciously homemade, with little to no packaging and half the cost. We won't cut corners next time.

Scratch cooking isn't as hard as we think it is. And it's so worth it in the end. We have been eating clean and homemade food for months, and this situation was an eye-opener. Many people always eat packaged food, but if they had a few months to make food themselves and then returned to packaged food, they would be shocked by the contrast. None of us felt that good after the party.

Chapter Eight

Building A Sanctuary By Hand

Arthur, the house, is 123 years old right now. I'm sure it was a house for a mining family. We are very close to a historic mining park and museum. This mine shut down in 1956, transforming the town into a historic tourist attraction. It has also attracted a lot of affluent retirees and city folk. Our house was purchased at a decent price, as I discussed in a previous chapter, but it is now worth almost double that price. I am grateful that we bought Arthur when we did because today, we wouldn't be able to afford to even walk through this neighborhood and dream.

I have been on this painting kick this year. When we moved in, we painted every room with leftover paint from the other house and paint given to us by friends or neighbors. We mixed and played, but most of the house was either washed-out yellow or light blue. One day, while walking Molly, I found free paint, and the next morning, I painted an accent wall of warm reddish-orange in the kitchen; then, with the smaller can of paint, I did the backboard and behind the counters with an Earthy rust color. I loved it so much that I couldn't wait to wake up and brew my coffee in what felt like a new kitchen. It had been a pale yellow, and now it was vibrant. That is when I started looking through colors and buying paint. Before the New Year, I had a little extra cash, and I bought all sorts of paint in rich colors: Herb Garden Green, Fields of Gold, Tuscan Yellow. I bought some at the Hardware store and purchased Espresso and Ocean Blue at Habitat For Humanity's store. I have been repainting all the rooms since the beginning of 2024. My living room is a gorgeous green, my office a warm mustard, and the rest of the kitchen is Tuscan yellow. I'll be painting one of the bedrooms, the Ocean Blue, and the pantry, the Espresso.

Paint can almost completely transform a house. There are ways to get free paint. I've found so much on Craigslist, but I wasn't in the mood back then. Neighbors and friends always seem to have some collecting dust in the garage. I wanted specific colors this time, so I had to pay. I spent $250 at the hardware store and $50 at the HFH store.

I have purchased a few rugs on Amazon and Home Depot for very little. I am cautious because some rugs fall apart quickly, but I did find a lovely Oriental rug knock-off on Amazon for $160, and after years of vacuuming and shampooing, it still looks good and hasn't unraveled. So, I found a similar one for the office at $150 and another for one of the bedrooms at $89. I find that the rugs at my thrift stores are blah, and they have them laid out on the floor being walked on all day, so they are filthy, and they wanted almost $200. It was cheaper to buy new.

Another item I purchased was a 52-inch TV for all the movies we love. It was a generic brand with no HD (which I don't care for anyway), and it was not too big, just big enough. I just wanted something more significant than the 32-inch we used to have. I love my Avengers and Marvel, and I need Thor to be on a bigger screen. The TV cost $235 at Walmart and is a Roku, which is fantastic. We can watch many free shows and movies, and I love playing Pandora music all day while working.

I bought a fancy new washing machine seven years ago during a Fourth of July sale. I thought it broke down once, and I washed our clothes in the bathtub until one day, a former realtor of ours texted me out of the blue and offered me her old washer and dryer they needed to get rid of. Now, for whatever reason, my washer works again, but I kept the dryer in the house and stored the washer in our shed just in case we have another "episode." Washing jeans and linens in the tub was no picnic, but it did give me complete respect for our great-grandmothers. They must have had powerful biceps.

I have a $700 laptop, and that includes a three-year warranty. I used to buy cheap, refurbished laptops for $100, but they kept breaking down, so we splurged. I have made a lot of money on this laptop. I've edited my videos and written a few books.

I bought some Pioneer Woman pot and pan sets, a crockpot, and a salt and pepper shaker. I bought two fancy stoneware nonstick pans recently because Pioneer Woman pans suck after a couple of years. And I bought a $50 bread maker because I use it almost daily to make wheat bread for morning toast.

As for everything else, I have decorated the whole house with free furniture and cooking tools, art, small area rugs, pantry shelves, dishes, cups, books, and lamps. I've found it all on the street or Craigslist. We even picked up a free Marcy Home Gym that fits nicely in the corner of the bedroom. We are on a massive health food, and fitness kick right now, so we have a small and compact elliptical in my office, a stationary bike in the living room, and now the home gym in the bedroom. And we do use them all every day, believe it or not. I did buy the elliptical after our $40 thrift store elliptical finally broke down. After searching, I bought the elliptical and bike for under $700 combined.

Our living room has a beautiful floral futon couch in an oak frame that was never used and free, a leather recliner, a bohemian coffee table, and some plant stands with huge, lush plants, all free. One side table was free; the other was $20 on the street. The kitchen has a free round antique table and free chairs, a free stove, and wooden shelves that we pulled out of a side room, and I painted barn red with paint my neighbor gave me. Free. I have a single Frigidaire bought cheaply, and it has lasted years. The pantry has free shelves and cheap shelves bought at Home Depot years ago, a free dryer, and an old washer that likes to play dead and a free microwave. The bedrooms are filled with free bed frames, box springs, and mattresses that were never used (I don't want used mattresses or over-stuffed furniture. That can be gross), big wooden shelves, nightstands, and dressers. All free. My office has a big, oak, antique teacher's desk I found on the street, along with tall, wooden shelves, small dark wood shelves, a 32-inch TV, and an old swivel chair with pale pink cloth upholstery. Free. All free.

I forgot the espresso maker with milk foamer I found free on the street. It was still unopened in its box, and it was such a great and glorious day when I found it!

Our closets are filled with clothes we purchased at garage sales or thrift stores, even free garments I have found. We used to visit a Savers Thrift store less than two hours away when they sent me notices with 50% off all the clothing. Two years ago, maybe a little longer, I received that notice. My family and I drove down there with $500 and shopped till we dropped. I stocked up on three years' worth of boys' clothes for Summer, Winter, Fall, and Spring.

I bought pajamas, jeans, t-shirts, long-sleeved shirts, coats, light jackets, thermals, hats, scarves, backpacks, shorts, play clothes, dress clothes, and school clothes. I bought clothes for Bali and me, a quilt, bathroom rugs, toys, puzzles, and books. That $500 dressed my kids entirely for over two years. This is the third year, and I still have some clothes and lots of nice jackets and warm coats that will fit them into their late teens. This Summer, I filled in the thinning wardrobe with a huge box of clothes from my neighbor's garage sale. She has a son who is a little taller than my boys, and he had just outgrown his wardrobe. There were so many lovely, clean clothes in great shape. I then hit the local Goodwill and bought stacks of perfectly fitting jeans and button-up shirts. I spent $40 at the garage sale and $68 at Goodwill, and we now have an entire wardrobe to last another year or so. My kids dress very well. Sometimes, they look very trendy and hip.

I have also decorated the windows with curtains I got for free or at a garage sale, thrift store, and some at Big Lots.

It has taken a few years, and I have worked hard to donate and give away truckloads of furniture and belongings. I have searched streets, garage sales, and Craigslist to redecorate my home completely. When we first moved here, the furniture didn't fit in this house. The rooms were small and square, and I had big, chunky furniture. I gave it all away and found better furnishings for this house. I love to change things and switch up the decor now and then. I have no guilt, as all my furniture has always been hand-me-downs. I got it for free and then gave it away for free. Then I found other free stuff people were getting rid of. I have recycled and repurposed for years, giving furniture a second, third, and fourth life and home.

I get bored quickly, but repainting a room with a new color or rearranging the whole house can bring such a delightful freshness to the home. It is also a great way to deep clean as you pull everything out and move it around.

This year there will be no buying anything. We have an overabundance of stuff. Kyle Cease made a video about abundance, and he talked about how most of us have so much stuff that we could easily live a year without needing to buy anything. Back in the 70s, families didn't shop that much at all. The average family, be they low-income or middle-income, didn't change out their furniture, they didn't shop at malls all day, we didn't have online shopping, we had the 10 lb. Sears catalog. We would look through it and dream and circle everything we wanted. If we needed something, we would fill out a card, write a check, and send it off. It took 8 to 10 weeks to get it in the mail. It was all a slow, long process. Sometimes, we had to save up for an item. It could take a year of saving, dreaming, and waiting for a toy or kitchenware. We bought only essentials: groceries and school or summer clothes. Buying school or summer clothes meant buying only a few items to mix and match or getting hand-me-downs if you had older friends and family.

My mother had the same furniture from before I was born to the day she died. I even have a Wok that was hers and must be 70 years old. I also have one of her cast iron pans, which is just as old.

So, when I heard Kyle Cease talk about us going a year or more without having to buy anything, it felt different from people talking about "no spend years." Those feel depraved and depressing, but looking at it in the light, we have so much abundance already; why not just use what we have and be creative? That felt playful and doable.

No More Over Working And Burn Out

I used to be that woman who always worked like a farm horse. I would deep clean the whole house from stem to stern one day, plant a whole garden the next day, drive out of town to hit WinCo, do a colossal pantry stock-up shopping the day after, and spend the next day putting it all away and jarring all the bulk foods. After a week of work like this, I would spend days writing, editing, and filming while doing the daily sweeping, cooking, and bed-making. I was busy all the time, from sunrise to way past sunset.

And then I burnt out. Over and over and over. I'd rest a few days or a week, shake it off, and go back at it. I did a lot of things but not well, just ok. I will say that what Bali and I accomplished over the past few years has made things easier. For example, we worked in the gardens, planted cover crops, amended them with horse manure we had to haul in, and built compost piles. We spent years planting fruit and nut trees, berry vines, and bushes. We put up an above-ground pool we found for $350 at Habitat For Humanity and a patio with a pergola. We rebuilt the bathroom and foundation and fixed old electric wiring and plumbing.

The payoff is that I don't blow a fuse when I plug in the milk frother while the bread maker is going. We finally have flourishing gardens from which we can eat and save our health and money. Every year, we have more fruits and nuts. We have a second bathroom, which can be a miracle saver when you have four people in the house. We have a pool in the summer for playing, exercising, and keeping cool. We have a patio where I love to sit under the pergola and read novels and BBQ. I am excited about summer. That pool and patio have created this vacation resort feel. It has completely transformed our summers.

So, in short, there is a time to work like a dog, but only if it leads to a goal. The goal should make your life easier, such as working two jobs to pay off debt or working a job and going to school at night to get a degree to get a better job. Working hard for a few summers to get the garden up and going so you have free organics. Working and saving intensely to buy a fixer-upper so you never have to deal with rising rents and landlords again. These are examples.

And then you rest. Build a life that makes the future more manageable for you. Some people get on the treadmill of work and never get off. They work 60 hours a week year after year and never experience a calm, slow life. For some, this may be how they like it. If you have a career you love, it's not like work, so that is different. But when you work for someone else, building their business and fortune only to be discarded in the end, well, that can cause some severe depression. I believe a lot of people experienced that during the quarantine in

2020. Many people were let go overnight from jobs they had poured their lives into.

I can't advise anyone as to what to do. I only know my story, and I've been a workhorse all my life. I was raised to work hard from a young age; I started working at the age of 15 years in a convalescent home, went on to work as a Buser in a steak house, and then worked two jobs and went to school or worked three jobs seven days a week for the rest of my twenties and thirties. When I settled into my new role as a homemaker and mother, I enjoyed it but became a little bored initially. I was used to working and running around being busy. Before my first son was a year old, Bali's job shut down, and I opened a daycare to help pay the bills. That was work. But then we moved to another county for work and settled into a ranch house on a fruit farm by the river. Bali worked long hours as a cashier, and we lived on a small paycheck. I decided against opening another daycare when I got pregnant with our second and last son. I tried babysitting but quickly decided I would rather learn frugality and focus on my children than hustle little jobs here and there. I had waited over 40 years to have children and wanted to enjoy motherhood.

That was a lovely time. I focused on housekeeping for two years, cooking all our meals and adoring my babies. I vacuumed, nursed, tidied, made simple casseroles, created little play spaces, played music, had rituals and routines for the toddler and infant and myself. I hung laundry outside, had a small grocery envelope, read **The Complete Tightwad Gazette** cover to cover, and we lived by the seasons. It was a farming community, so everyone lived and worked by the seasons. The days were slow and pleasant. I didn't write during that time, I was never on the internet, and we only had an antenna that picked up a few channels such as PBS for kids, a classic movie station, and some black and white westerns.

We made very little, and the rent comprised almost 50% of our earnings. However, we had no debt, no credit cards, and one paid-off car. We foraged free wood in orchards where they were replacing old nut or fruit trees to burn in our wood stove to reduce the usage of the house heater. Propane was expensive, and the central heat and air vents were on the ceiling, so it took a lot to heat or cool the house. I used the wood stove mostly, and in the summer, I used fans and the whole house fan in the evenings to cool the house down. I hung out the laundry and packed all of Bali's lunches. I used a grocery envelope for monthly shopping. I nursed and used cloth diapers for a short time, but back then, we didn't have all the great videos on YouTube on how to clean them and avoid big messes by lining them. The minute one child had diarrhea, I stopped, sadly. Cloth diapers save a fortune. I started baking my bread, and casseroles were cheap to make, they were fabulous comfort food. I learned how to use the library to the fullest, ordering books all over the connecting counties and towns and spending my quiet time reading stacks of novels. I never shopped online or in town. We had more than enough. We had many baby clothes, from infant to 3 years old, that I had stocked up at thrift stores, and friends gave us hand-me-downs. I had a room full of toys from the daycare I previously had, as well as toys and music, and a bookcase full of children's books I had purchased at thrift stores and Craigslist.

We rarely went out, and if we did, it was for ice cream at the little ice cream parlor in the tiny historic river town, or we would go to Hometown Buffet when we did our shopping on Sunday in the big town half an hour away.

Friends would stay with us, and I'd cook up a storm. We would all enjoy playing at home and being together. We would take long drives because there was a lot of beautiful countryside, farms with orchards and vineyards, and historic towns to enjoy. We would play "tourist" for enjoyment. Taking drives was something Bali and I enjoyed doing.

Life was simple. We lived on very little back then. We were comfortable and wanted for nothing because we didn't want any more than we had. There were gifts every day. I was a new mother, filled with gratitude and love; because I was in my 40s, I thought it would never happen, and now I had two healthy boys. I enjoyed my morning coffee, the birds thick in the orchards, fussing happily over my infant and toddler, reading good novels in the backyard, playing with the dogs, watching the tractors and hay balers roll by on the upper road, harvest time and the pickers talking and playing music and the clanking of the ladders in the orchards, and the coyotes hunting at night. Everything had a rhythm.

We stayed there for two years. After that, we moved to a quiet city and lived in a smaller, cheaper house with fewer utilities. Bali had a better job, making a couple of dollars more an hour, and we were saving $600 on rent and utilities a month. I started a writing career, and on one of our trips to Costco to restock our pantry,

Bali bought me a $300 HP laptop. I wrote prolifically for the first two years. I wrote plain, frugal books and clumsy fiction, but I worked hard and read every popular author and genre.

Then, we went on to buy our first house, the HUD house, for $135K. We worked on that house for three years, and the last year, we worked and saved like crazy to buy this final house up in this historic mountain town. Did it make sense to leave a cute house with a tiny mortgage? Yes, because I wasn't happy there, and I found our dream town and a fantastic life up here, and I knew it was the best place for all of us. I wasn't wrong. We are all thriving, and we love where we live. Yes, it costs a bit more, but we also made more. Bali and I pool our little money; it is enough every month. Loosely mimicking the words of Jim Carrey, "We have enough, we did enough, we are now feeling like we are enough."

Another significant insight I have had lately was reading **The Three Waves Of Volunteers** with Dolores Cannon. At the back of the book, there is a part where Dolores works with a woman under hypnosis. Her Subconscious was sharing the wisdom through her. It's like when Esther Hicks channels Abraham, a group of spirits able to communicate by being channeled. They were talking about changes coming and being prepared and that we are all like our own Universe, and we experience it in our bodies, and I'm assuming our minds. What we put in our minds and bodies is crucial to our happiness and ability to serve others and the Earth. If we keep ourselves balanced and content, that energy goes out and heals. We don't need to get out the pop-up podium and preach or write novels on the subject or make vlogs droning on; we learn to make a lovely Universe in our space, and it goes out to others who are ready.

Here is what Christine or her guides were saying about this:

"All you need to do is focus here (the body), creating your heaven on Earth. Each human being is creating their heaven on Earth. That's all you have to do—come together with others to create their heaven on Earth and expand that energy. And before you know it, you've changed the world. You don't even think about the world. What you focus on is what you create. Think about peace. The main thing people have to understand is that what they focus on expands. So, if they focus on, if they can replace predictions with something wonderful they want, expand that. Then, they can create their heaven on Earth."

I agree, and I understand at last. We heal each other and the world and spread light by becoming a happy, calm person who feels content in their life. We clean up, heal ourselves (our Universe), and show this example. We spark a light for others without awareness. We often help others without knowing it. Every time we leave the house, we can inspire and help without knowing it. By being ourselves and showing kindness, gratitude, humor, and motivation, you ignite others and send healing energy to everyone. By focusing on positive thoughts and replacing negative ideas and beliefs with new, wholesome ideas and beliefs that serve everyone and everything, you mend the tears in the fabric of our history, communities, and individuals. We work as spirits, so we aren't always aware of this work. It's a big one to wrap our minds around, but we need to for our well-being and everyone around us. We must be happy with ourselves, and only we can do that ourselves.

It may seem we got off track, but we haven't. What *you* need is none of my business. But I need a good, rich, happy, blessed life. I have that now that I've given up everything I thought was what I needed or wanted for a great life. Even in the last two weeks, my idea of what I needed in prosperity and success has changed profoundly. I wanted to be a super successful, famous writer and make a fortune. Recently, since the healings with the Tibetan Monks, I'm not feeling it anymore. I don't want all that money, which might unnecessarily change things. What do I genuinely want, then? I want to be comfortable. I want to have enough financial flow to enjoy organic foods, go to the movies when I want, buy used books at the fabulous used bookstore downtown, go out to lunch or a latte now and then, or hit the thrift store and have a little shopping spree. I want to donate heavily to projects focusing on reforestation, helping animals and children, and supporting Indigenous people. I want to hire help in the future for work on the house, and when I'm swamped writing, I hire someone to clean sometimes. And replace a vehicle when it dies one day. We do have some crazy miles on the car and truck, after all. I would be happy with just one car and continuing to walk most places when the weather permits. Everyone should have a walkable town. One of character and color, if not history and natural beauty. When you have a lovely town to walk in, even if it's a little worn in parts, walking to the market for some fruit can be a nice trip on foot. And we would love to travel.

With my revelations as of lately, I don't feel this urgency to make money now. I enjoy being frugal and reading my old books, not just TCTWG. Still, I have another one about mothers choosing to stay home and overcoming a lack of money or making it through times of unemployment with the breadwinner. It shares their ways of saving money and making that slight paycheck stretch twice as much. They talk about how important it has been having the mother at home full-time and how it's kept the family together. This goes for the husband or other partner, as well. It is essential that we can all stay together peacefully, no matter the challenges that come. The book is **The Heart Has Its Reasons** by Mary Ann Cahill.

I feel like it's always essential, be it the man or woman, that the most capable and nurturing parent be home or come home. Even if your child or children are teens now and you think it's too late, believe me, they need you just as much as when they were little, despite them not showing it maybe. And even if you have no children, just a spouse and a dog, it's still essential. You are there to support the breadwinner and nurture that dog or cat. Seems silly? I think it's silly we chase money and work so hard to buy things we don't need. There are so many things we could stop buying, get rid of, and downsize, so we don't need that much money and don't have to chase and hustle. We need to live frugally and wisely.

I read a book compiled of blogs from a woman who was poor all her life. She had five or six kids and dealt with a husband who had some real issues and kept running off and leaving her to raise the kids alone. He finally did come home permanently; it seems he had worked through his demons and was able to be stable, provide, and be there for the family for the next 26 years until he passed. When he was gone, she was on government assistance. She was unhappy to be on this; other women would give her a hard time and tell her to get her life in order and work. But she wanted to be with her children, caring for and watching over them. Not a daycare provider or a nursery school. We all may have different feelings about this, but I understand and respect her need to be with her children 100%, even if it did mean government assistance for a time. When her husband finally came to roost permanently, he didn't make much money; I feel he may have been working minimum wage and sometimes with tips, depending on his job. Sometimes, he didn't have work for a short period. But she remained home, and they agreed that he would work outside the home, and she would be in the home and raise the children. She didn't rush out to find a job, no matter how difficult it got. She stayed steady, cooked a wholesome meal, and kept the children's routines. She never spoke of poverty, and she talks about how her kids thought they had money until later when they went to school and met other kids from all sorts of financial backgrounds. I loved her stories of simple living and getting by. They have comfort and family in them. Some parts are inspiring and fortifying in deciding to be home despite hardships. I would have loved it if she went into great detail about how she made it on so little, kept a roof over their heads, and kept them clothed and fed. She only tells bits and pieces.

She talks about how much she and her girlfriends, who were also poor with children, loved a squeaky-clean house; poor as it may be, it was immaculate. They pretended they had it all together and made the best of everything. Her husband had bought her and the kids a house for $20K back in the 70s, and I'm not sure how she paid for it or if he had paid in full, but despite it being old and having bugs, she was grateful to have a roof, warm beds for her children, and a kitchen. I love how she would break it down to basics that we take for granted. She got rid of the water bugs herself by using some natural powder. She homeschooled for years, and she never drove. She had a huge garden out back, canned and preserved from it. She could make things stretch.

The book is **Dear Kitchen Saints** by Connie Hultquist. I will caution that she is hardcore religious and anti-feminist. I don't jive with her religious outlook, or her anti-feminist take. It sometimes upsets and annoys me, but we take the stuff we like and leave the rest. To each their own. I am amazed at her endurance in staying in a marriage that was so hard in the beginning, and fortunately for her and the kids, the husband showed up one day and never left. He has done an excellent job in almost three decades. I must ignore everything I don't agree with to enjoy her simplicity of life and homemaking and her absolute devotion to her kids. And her children seemed to have turned out well and happy. A devoted mother is all I need to hear about, and I need to hear how she made things work when there wasn't much to work with.

We live in a day and age of working hard and two-income families. To each his own, and in that respect, I decide to be home and live calmly, to be pleasant and comfortable, and to be here for my kids until they are grown. Even then, I will be here because motherhood is not done when the kids leave home. Motherhood goes on forever until we pass on to the next life.

Chapter Ten

Affording The Gift Of Staying Home

Yesterday, we bought a box full of organic produce for juicing. For $34, we had a big box full of onions (not for juicing), apples, cucumbers, beets with beet greens, ginger, carrots, and cucumbers. It made almost two gallons of rich, healthy juice that we store in the fridge and drink daily. There is a very inspiring story on YouTube of a man's father who was overweight; he had gone vegan and was riding his bike to work and home every day. He had been juicing for years, and when he had his blood work done, the doctors were amazed that such an overweight man could have such great stats on blood pressure and cholesterol. This was before he went vegan and started losing weight. He swore by his juicing every single morning.

Juicing is a process, so we juice a considerable batch one day a week. It fills a bucket with compost and makes gallons of juice, and it takes a couple of hours to wash and juice all the veggies, fruit, and greens. But when we drink a big jar of it in the morning, it feels like pure life coming into our bodies instead of the ordinary dead, cooked things that taste so delicious but do more harm than good.

Let me share this tidbit if you think health food is too expensive. Green juice can cost from $7 to $10 at the health food store. I found Buda Juice, a raw and organic green juice, for $11 online. You can get cheap green juices for $3, but they aren't fresh or organic and are loaded with sugar.

Our fresh, organic, raw juice loaded with beets, beet greens, lemon, ginger, apples, cucumbers, celery, and carrots cost us $1.70 for 16 oz. The health food store would start at $7.99 or $9.99, but if we added everything we have here, it would be up to maybe $12.99 for 16 oz.

If you are good at math and love breaking down price points, you could figure out how much it costs to make a homemade lasagna or loaf of bread or coffee and so on. I can make a vegan latte with two espresso shots for a dollar, but if I get it at Starbucks, it's $4.75 or more. I can make organic wheat bread for a dollar or buy it for $6 at the health food store. I can make a gallon of organic soy milk for .50 cents or buy it for $4.99 a half gallon at the coop. Some things are much cheaper, such as a box of mac and cheese, but the taste and quality are not to be compared. The boxed and canned meals and soups are rarely as good as homemade.

Most of the time, homemade food is much cheaper and tastes superior to the factory-made foods calling us from their store shelves. Store-bought food has so many chemicals and preserves that it lasts forever. A lady overheard me at the grocery store encourage my son to buy fresh avocadoes and make homemade guacamole. I said, "It takes so much better if it is fresh and without the weird stuff." The lady agreed; she said her guacamole lasted too long for her comfort, "It doesn't go bad like fresh fruits and vegetables are supposed to." And she said her daughter had a loaf of bread that lasted months and wasn't moldy. I didn't ask what sort of bread; maybe it was the real junky white stuff, but this woman is right about things lasting too long. If I buy butter from the store, I can leave it out forever, and it never goes wrong. If I make vegan butter from scratch, if left out, it goes bad within days. That is a good sign. Natural food should turn and mold and rot. That's natural. Organic produce shouldn't be perfect and free of bug holes. Bugs mean organic. Bugs won't eat chemicals, so why should we?

We planted gardens and an orchard not because we think there will be such hard times ahead but because planting and growing our food ensures 100% organic and saves thousands of dollars in fresh produce. We also reduce our carbon footprint by not having to buy food that has traveled. It travelled a few yards from the garden to the kitchen, with no gasoline required. We have such rich soil now that our food is loaded with vitamins and minerals. As my friend jokes using gaming terminology, if we were in a computer game, we would level up our health to a whole new level. We're like gorillas when it comes to eating produce. We could go through boxes of it every few days. We grow a food forest, flowers, trees, and bushes. We have created a rich ecosystem in our yard. Our yard was a quarter acre of clay dirt, weeds, and a few overgrown fruit trees, but now it is lush, with rich soils and strong growing trees. We have swarms of bees, birds of every kind year-round, my pet squirrels, a skunk family, and a fox. All are welcome.

That is a significant way we make it work on minimum wage. Of course, the minimum wage in California is more significant than in most places. And I have royalties from books. But people spend a lot of money on food and gas for the cars. We live within a 3 to 6-mile radius of everything in our town and the next town. We walk to many activities. So, we grow food, eat simple plant-based, and drive very little. This saves hundreds a month.

Our mortgage is half of our income, which I wouldn't suggest. I agree with the old-fashioned idea that your shelter should be no more than 30% of your income. But on the bright side, you can live comfortably even if your shelter is half your income. You know the drill: no debt, credit cards, or car payments. It's the only way to live. It's hard to find the discipline to pay off debts, cars, and houses, but it is a game changer. That's what my friends who have paid off their homes tell me. Imagine having no debt; how sweet that must be. And to own your house right out. You'll still pay taxes and insurance, but you own it, and without a mortgage, the taxes and insurance should be very doable.

I've signed us up with some programs that reduce energy bills, such as CARE with PG & E. Recently, we signed up with ACP to have our internet bill reduced by half. We use our medical for dental visits for the kids. I get a huge discount because I pay cash.

I have a lot of books on natural healing and homeopathic remedies, **Dr. Earl Mindell's Vitamin Bible**, and a few books from **Prescription For Nutritional Healing and Prescription For Herbal Healing**. I have Dr. Gregers **How Not To Die**. This saves money because we are very healthy. We eat well, exercise plenty, drink lots of clean water as our main beverage, take vitamins, and maintain a life free of worry and stress by not watching the news and living an easy life that doesn't require power jobs with corporations.

I study and learn all I can about nutrition without getting too complicated. It isn't hard to figure out: lots of clean, fresh, whole foods, primarily fruits and vegetables, legumes, lentils, nuts, seeds, whole grains, and water—everything from the Earth, trees, and vines.

I dive into my homemaking books often to focus on thrift, feel gratitude, and remember how good we have it these days. I read books like **When The Banks Closed, We Opened Our Hearts, We Had Everything But Money, Touch Times, and Strong Women.** These books are filled with stories from the Depression Era. They are stories of ingenuity, overcoming hardships, family, and a time when so many had so little but still found the good in things and had a lot of gratitude. These are inspiring stories, and after reading a few, I remember how MUCH we have, how fortunate we are, and how well we live and thrive. I also become more focused on making things stretch, making do, and finding free "wanted things" and sometimes essentials. I think ahead, and when money comes into our lives, I sit with it for a few days before deciding how to use it to serve us best and longest.

I want to read this from **The Heart Has Its Reasons**. This is from Cindy George, "If you could buy something for your children that would make their early years the happiest and give them a super head start, wouldn't you go into debt for it?" This was her reply when people didn't understand why she wasn't out trying to get a job with her secretarial skills. "But we truly believe that by my being home, we are also investing substantially in our children's future happiness."

If we have children, it makes sense to invest in them by giving them the one thing they want the most: parents who are present and involved.

If you're reading this book, you are trying to figure something out. You are not entirely content but, on the way, reading, watching, or listening to any guidance that will help you get where you need to be. Some books had considerable effects on how I changed things in the last couple of years: **Essentialism** by Greg McKeown, **What Falls From The Sky** by Esther Emery, and one that doesn't seem inspiring, but it was for me, **Evicted: Poverty and Profit in the American City** by Matthew Desmund.

I've gone into these books in other talks, so I won't be repetitive, but each one helped me to unplug more and let more people, places, and things go. The Evicted book gave me a hard kick around money and showed me how we must always be wise and frugal to thrive and have plenty. We also need to make careful choices and not be controlled by addictions or other people. We are very focused on paying off our house, and I believe more than ever that owning your home is so important, but it must be affordable, a mortgage that is easy to pay for 30 years or quicker—that way, you aren't a slave to some landlord and the rising rents. I have a friend who pays $1550 for a two-bedroom apartment with only a balcony facing the back of Dollar General. Every year, her rent is raised by 7%. You can guess that as the rent goes up, up, up, the 7% grows too. Knowing that your budget will be even tighter each year is stressful. I want some stability with my shelter. I want the same mortgage year after year and one day not to have a mortgage.

This life can be done, but it takes an open mind, the ability to be creative and disciplined, the ability to work hard at some times and slow down at other times, and the ability to be positive and strong of mind, choosing a healthy mind and body over everything. We have chosen stability over partying, going out, traveling, and doing all the fun things everyone else is doing, but we now have a sanctuary where we can rest, play, learn, and heal for the rest of our lives. Now that we have built a strong life, we can eventually travel and play a little. Frugality helps you save enough money to do great things.

I have frugal friends who are rich and own half a town. I have friends who live out of their cars but always have money for fun and play. Sobriety and wise investments seem to win out. But there is a fine line with all these scenarios.

Learn all you can about frugality and thrift. Then practice it. It takes a year to learn and perfect, and I've been doing it for decades, but I still have to pull myself back in and make it fun and exciting. I love spending money and going here and there. I would like to see more financial flow down the road so I can take the kids on trips to other countries and we can do more living outside our home. We are starting to do that now, but in little increments. My kids do so much through their school; plays at local theaters, travel to other cities, and have all sorts of dances and parties. I have my little shopping sprees when the thrift store a few streets over has 50% off at the beginning of every month. The local movie house has flashback movie nights for $5. There is a way to have a lot of good times with less cash. No need to be bored or deprived.

Chapter Eleven

Do I Get Bored At Home?

I have never been bored a day in this life. At first, yes. When Arjan was first born, and I went from working all the time to being home, I did go through some awkwardness. But I had many friends and would visit my old work or have coffee with a girlfriend. I could walk everywhere, and my friends would have potlucks and gatherings, so there was always something social. When we moved to the fruit farm by the river, three hours from my friends and community, I did feel a bit lonely and bored, but it shifted quickly. I was pregnant again and thrilled to have another child in my 40s. I had thought my dreams of having a child would never happen when I celebrated my 40th birthday, but here I was, 43 years old, and had an adorable toddler and another on the way. My joy overcame my sadness at leaving the ocean and my girlfriends.

That was a crucial time. I learned to slow down and be present. It was a farming community, so I started to go with the seasons and the sun and moon, just like everyone around me. I learned to live in quiet and be content with slow days. I took up reading, and I read like crazy. I ordered stacks of novels from the tiny library across the street from Bali's work. I started practicing more frugality, which I found fun and still do. I never get sick of it. I don't enjoy the millions of frugal videos on YouTube, but I still love the frugal books in my library. I still pour over them to be wiser. We can always be wiser still.

That time on the fruit farm was the quietest and slowest time. Eventually, some friends from our old community would stay with us, and I reunited with an old high school friend who lived nearby and was also a homemaker and would come out once a week to visit. Then, I would go into town and grocery shop with her once a week. She was the one who taught me about WinCo and had a membership at Costco so that we could stock up from there now and then. She and I made our first bucket of homemade laundry soap. Life had small gifts and lots of quiet time baking in the Summer evenings, getting back to reading copiously as I used to as a youth, long Sunday drives through corn fields, pear, and cherry orchards, past alfalfa and vineyards, discovering little historic towns, some just hanging on by old beams and bolts.

I never did well in school or college. I was never as interested as desperately as I wish I had been. However, now I homeschool myself, and I love learning. I study everything and anything that interests me; some things fascinate me, and I study for years. I have learned more in my years as a homemaker and mother than I ever did in all the wasted years at community colleges. I have done more and learned more these years than in all the schools **and** all the jobs.

I'm busy every day studying films, which, yes, I do, if you're snickering. I don't just watch films; I study them, watching parts repeatedly because I'm learning to spin stories, build characters, and think in another dimension. A fictional writer must learn to open the mind to all possibilities and worlds. I tell myself daily to 'just observe, don't judge or step in, just observe people, situations, interactions.' This helps to tell stories. Everywhere I go, there are possible stories.

I read a lot of books. I'm always in the middle of reading a few books at a time. Gardening books, fictional mysteries, thrillers or history, cookbooks, love those, spiritual, aliens, frugal, or homemaking. I get into it all. I love watching cooking videos and maybe a little gardening. I used to watch videos for everything; it was great, but now I try to turn to my books to learn or be reinspired.

I sometimes crotchet, just one stitch, now two, because I just learned how to make the dishwashing rags. I can make blankets, scarves, and dish rags. Not perfectly, they all look like a kid did the work, but I enjoy making them while watching movies and between writing to get focused and centered. I feel accomplished when I have a scarf to add to the closet or a rag for my dishes. I haven't done a blanket in forever. I mend things; mostly, we leave the mending to the man of the house. He mends all our things. He just mended this little hole in my puffy jacket. I love it so much. I got hooked on some wire or fence part.

My writing is all-consuming in its own way. My kids are the other all-consuming part.

I have taken up sketching and coloring. Very therapeutic.

I know my home inside out. I wash, fuss, dust, and rearrange. We are lucky to live in a time when thrift stores and garage sales are abundant. For very little, I can fill my nest with warmth and comfort from second-hand shops.

My beauty treatments and routines cost so little, and I even have tools like the foot bath. I get them inexpensively online; I have glycolic peels, Retinal, Vitamin C, and Collagen. I get my hair dye from Grocery Outlet. I stock up when they have good blond colors. I keep stocked up on bath goods such as Epsom salts and Calgon. Remember, "Calgon, take me away." I love my baths in the winter, with the rain pouring down on the plastic roof over the shed off the bathroom and the warm twinkle lights. I also have a good book in a hot, bubbly bath. It's healing and soothing, and I usually spend a good hour reading, writing down ideas, and pondering everything in that tub. I'm like Trumbo without the typewriter. You, fellow film buffs, will get it.

I love to tidy. I love opening curtains, folding blankets, wiping counters, and straightening things out. Cleaning deeply is another adventure that needs a mindset and preparation, but I enjoyed it and love my house afterward. The clean smell and freshness of the washed floors and scoured bathroom. It is a ritual. First, I shower quickly because I must feel fresh and ready. It is strange to bathe before cleaning, but that is me. I put on comfortable clothes for optimal flexibility. I did this yesterday, and I observed the routine so I could write about it. I wore a comfortable t-shirt that is a little loose but not too loose and baggy, and you don't want to catch it on things or dip it in cleaning buckets. It has to fit. I wore pedal pusher stretch pants and my hair up from my face for complete visibility.

Then I put on music that raises my vibration. You may be laughing, but I'm not kidding; this is a big thing for me. The music must be uplifting and music that inspires thought. I think, reflect, heal, and clean my mind when working. I think of chapters for books, both my homemaking and my fictional. I think about how much I love our life and what I want to get out of it. I think about my parenting and how I can improve because I'm not even close to perfection yet. Maybe in a few more lifetimes. Ok, you got the music going; now put on another espresso pot of coffee and froth thick, creamy oat milk. This and date syrup are my two favorite things in coffee now. I don't do the flavored anymore. They gave me a slight headache, tasted too sweet, and were filled with chemicals, even if I watered them with plain plant milk.

Coffee is brewing, music is playing, and you have on your flexible, easy-to-move-in clothes. You now get out all the cleaning supplies. I use a broom, vacuum, steam mop, a small bucket with hot water and soap, gloves, old towels, and rags; all rags are made from old towels and t-shirts that weren't good enough to donate. I repurposed an old spray bottle filled with hot water, dish soap, and bleach. I use it on the floors when I steam mop to give it extra cleanliness. I will transition to vinegar instead of bleach because my old dogs are past now, and I had that robust solution because of them and the accidents. We don't wear shoes in this house, but the kids like to run around outside barefoot, and I encourage it. It's good for us to ground into the Earth. But then that Earth comes into the house. There is not much, but a little steaming is excellent.

I sweep and vacuum from stem to stern first, then put away the broom and vacuum—less clutter. Then, I do the nastiest jobs that I dread. The toilet is cleaned inside, outside, top to bottom, and around. I do use a bleach and soap solution in another repurposed spray bottle. The shower is laborious and requires a scrubber, sponge, and toothbrush. But it's my happy place, so I cleaned it to a sparkle. I throw all the little rugs in the wash with the cleaning rags and steam mop clothes, and wash them all after the job is complete. The rest of the work is easy. Steam mop the whole house, and sometimes I shampoo the large area rugs in the living room, office, and bedroom. I shampoo carpets when the weather is warm, and I can leave windows and doors open to dry them. Sometimes, I pull out the fridge, stove, washer and dryer, and chest freezer to clean behind and under. Not every time, but it gets nasty in those behind spots. I pull out furniture, and what collects behind and under couches and beds is impressive. When the kids were little, there were piles of Legos in every imaginable space.

When I'm done, the place feels so good, and I feel good. That is one way I keep busy and happy.

My writing is all-consuming in my sectioned-off writing world. I have the mom and homemaker world and then the writing world, but the two do sometimes meet and meld. I have a shelf loaded with writing how-to books; some I've read, some I've skimmed, some collect dust. I watch writing videos just because I love to. Writing and cooking videos are my favorite. I put a recording app on my phone so when I'm out and about and think of something, I can record it. I record in the car and on the trails. Those thoughts don't always make it home; you know what I'm saying. The brain can be like a colander; great ideas drain out before you get to the keyboard or pencil and paper. I join NaNoWriMo every year. I don't always finish, but I love November and zealously jump in. I have dictionaries, vocabulary builders, thesaurus, and a dictionary of synonyms and antonyms. Reading old literature is the best way to learn new words. They wrote and spoke in a lost way, but the fancy words can be sprinkled in any book to spruce it up. I prefer using a paper dictionary because it's so hard to find the word that you never forget how to spell it and you find other words on the way to that word.

I write all morning, after chores, and before making the main supper. I love being in my office, filled with everything I enjoy: movies with my old TV, books, and my laptop. I sit at my desk and half-watch a movie while reading and writing little bits here and there. It is an all-day affair sometimes. I recently suffered writer's block and wasn't doing any of this. I just needed to rest and move away from making YouTube videos. I needed to regain my energy and be quiet for a few months.

And now I'm back to my old writing wizard self. I derive a lot of happiness from this work.

I might be bored and lonely if I did the basics of a homemaker/mom. If I just cleaned the house on a schedule, never moved the furniture, never played with paint or decorating from garage sales and free stuff, if I cooked the same dishes every week in the same order: pizza on Friday, soup on Monday…I would be very bored. If I tried to be perfect or be a fantastic homemaker like Martha Stewart, I'd be miserable. But I accept my limits and focus on what I enjoy and do well; I treat my house like a grown-up doll house and play so much with it. I play with the cooking all the time. We are always trying new recipes. We have favorites like pizza, stroganoff, and vegetable chow mien, but there is always a new sauce, baked good, or main dish. As I mentioned before, being plant-based has lifted my creativity level. It is like a whole new hobby.

I fuss over my kids, and now that they are older and not so much fussing is tolerated by them, I now avert my fussing over my little Molly, who is like having a baby without all that work. Still, she does have her bed that needs washing, her toys that I gather and organize after we play, I make homemade food and get turkey necks from the butcher, and she has her walks and baths; I trim her nails and play with her through the day. She gets her little massages and is tucked in for nap time. I know, it's all so silly for a dog, but she's so cute and five years old, but she's still very puppy-like. She looks at me with adoring brown eyes; the world is hers.

I'm never lonely. I have a handful of wonderful friends who are different yet on the same path. The variety in personalities is excellent for me. I have the best conversations with these ladies. They are kind, supportive, encouraging, inspiring, and seekers of spiritual truths and work, just like me. I have lengthy conversations some mornings with any one of them. But the most immense comfort is having my children here and the father. The house is complete, and I love having everyone present. I don't have the energy or desire to go out often. I had my party days, and I prefer to be home, safe, cozy, and surrounded by hobbies and fun things to do. On rainy days, we can be on the computer, doing art, reading, and watching shows and movies. Sometimes we play chess or checkers. In the

Summer, we swim, BBQ, and walk the trails in the forest. We hang out at the library still.

So, that sums it up. I wouldn't change anything. Money is abundant sometimes, and we stock up for the times it isn't, so it's always a steady lifestyle. I was worried about becoming a successful writer, but lately, I don't need to worry about that. I need to love what I write. That is the priority. The money will come; sometimes, it will overflow, and sometimes it will trickle. I still wake up and play and do chores, slurp coffee, nag, and laugh- just the same.

I put a lot of fun and love into this book, and I hope it ignites a spark in you to be free and happy and create your sanctuary. Don't be a slave to what we are "supposed to do, be, have." Find what you want to fill your soul up. It's probably in the forest.

Chapter Twelve

The End Of Poverty Consciousness

The other day, I was alone doing chores. The kids were at school, and I was bustling about cleaning the kitchen, making beds, and kneading dough in the kitchen. The opera was loud because I could only enjoy it when everyone was gone. Father is at work, kids at school, translates to mother + espresso + Opera = productivity. I was inspired to make homemade bread instead of using my bread maker. It has been a long time since I had a big bowl of dough rising in the kitchen. Bread doesn't rise as well in the winter; the kitchen can be a little crisp if I don't bring in the area heater. The central heat doesn't reach the kitchen or bathroom well, so we use Presto Heat dishes.

I had forgotten how therapeutic it is to mix dough and knead it. I had deep thoughts about my life: what I adored and what I wasn't so crazy about. Then I set up the dough in the bowl with a hot towel to help it rise (this seems to work great) and went to the bedrooms to make the beds. As I made the big bed, I felt a moment of gratitude for this cozy home, and I was amazed at how well we had done and how much we had accomplished with so little income. I have already filed taxes, and the letters from Medical said that we still qualify for full coverage. We made a little more last year, so I wasn't sure if we would need to start on Covered CA., a sliding scale insurance. Turns out we are still poor enough. This is a huge blessing. We don't use the insurance because we are crazy healthy, but I like having it for emergencies or updating kids' vaccines and dental visits twice a year. The clinics up here are all closed to new patients, so Bali and I pay cash at an office 30 miles away that gives us 50% discounts for cash payments.

I also received an application for CalFresh. CalFresh is food stamps in California. It turns out, according to the government, we are just that poor. This was when I had a channel. I don't make that money now, so things are a little tighter. With a husband making minimum wage (It's high in California, but so is the cost of living) and my book royalties dwindling because I've barely produced a book in a year and a half, it does get tight. And we still thrive.

But what I realized, standing in my sweet bedroom and enjoying my bohemian-decorated Victorian, smelling the espresso brewing in the kitchen, listening to Pavarotti sing Nessun Dorma with passion in my living room, is that we have a beautiful life, and it didn't cost much. I have never had access to a lot of money, and I watched my mother struggle with it in my childhood, so I know how to make magic happen with a few dollars and coins. I know now how to find so much good stuff for free or a fraction of the cost. We live in an affluent area, and I have filled my house with lovely furniture and art, which I found on Craigslist and on the street. Because I have learned to cook from scratch, we can eat many good foods that are expensive to buy premade or at a restaurant. My homemade café saves me $1,530 a year…honestly, double that at $3,060 because I have two a day most days. Maybe less if you count my cost of plant creamer, coffee, and date syrup, so at least $2,000 plus. My Berkey saves us up to $5,000 a year in jugs and bottles of water. All my cloth napkins, towels, cleaning rags from old cloths, steam mop, cloth menstrual pads, and reusable straws save $500 to $1000 a year depending on if you account for items such as Clorox wipes and swifter mop wet cloth refills. We are talking about savings of $8,000 or more just using cloth and reusables, making coffee at home, and having a water filter. Now, if you add in scratch cooking and reduce your dairy and meat, the more you do it, you are saving anywhere from $6000 to $12,000 a year extra, but this depends on whether you cut down on animal products and premade foods or you go hardcore into scratch cooking and plant-based whole foods. Then, if you only go out to eat once a month instead of weekly and start growing a big garden and planting a small orchard, you harvest more organic produce and nuts every year. We are talking thousands of dollars more! Oh my. The more steps you add and the deeper you go, the more you save. The less money going out and the easier life gets.

With everything we do to save money, from the tiniest and silliest things to the most significant things, I would say that we save $15,000 a year just by doing everything I mentioned. We could save more if I didn't order books and hit the thrift shops or grocery shops frequently. I tend to drop by the store for a couple of items and come out with a couple of bags of groceries. I know better, but it doesn't mean I can always follow the frugal laws or want to.

Since cutting back on my workload, I must be more careful. It's hitting home how small the budget is right now. I only shop when we have a few extra bucks and I get bulk foods and seasonings to ensure we have a good pantry and I can make many meals. I have stopped ordering books and now rely solely on the library. We don't shop any more unless it's a kids birthday.

I do have Spring to look forward to, with all that Spring cleaning and house purging everyone in the neighborhoods will be doing. Molly and I will find all sorts of treasures on the streets during our daily walks. I won't bring home just anything, as I have been doing some purging myself, but I will likely find a goodie here and there. My colorful Afghan on the back of the couch and the little green espresso machine were all treats I found on the street. If we had no money this whole time, I still would have filled this house with furniture, decor and art, cooking tools, books, and bedding from Craigslist and the streets. Our stove and microwave were from Craigslist, and our washer and dryer were from a former realtor. It's crazy all the good things you can find if you take the time to search and pay attention.

As much as I enjoy this life, working with a little budget doesn't bother me. It challenges me, and I turn it into a game. With every score or win, I feel a little victory. Decorating my home, filling my pantry, baking fantastic bread, and finding the funds for things for the kids make me feel good and accomplished.

I'm spending this time working hard on my writing. I have already published a fictional novel. I'm *not* making a big fuss about it because it's not fantastic. It's a light read for the train and was a way for me to get back into the fictional saddle. Writing is a joy and a hobby in my veins. I've been writing since I was little. I used to write and illustrate little fairy tales with princesses and castles with my crayons. I would cut the paper into little sheets and staple them together, making mini books. Then I went on to journal my life, my feelings, and the hardships living with my mother, who was mentally ill.

Every so many years, I would burn them all. There would be crates and boxes of these journals. I journaled about our trip while traveling Europe but lost my journals somewhere in Greece. When my mother was dying, and I moved up to her mountain cabin, I journaled daily about the experience of helping another person die peacefully and enter back into the Spirit world. I lost those entries when the laptop died. After my mother passed and I moved to town, I wrote a book about my whole life from birth to my thirties. I never kept it; I never wanted to publish it; it was just for me and deeply cathartic. I loved getting up early before work and writing every day. I wrote my book *Sober Queen* after a year of sobriety. I loved writing that book. Then, I took a break for a few years to date, marry, and become a housewife and mother. When I took up writing again, I never stopped. I wrote thirty-four books in less than eight years.

As you can see, it's what I do. I am no Cindy Woodsmall or Anne Lamott, but I love it and have had a little bit of success. I will keep writing and learning; one day, I may have more success.

I have faith, and I know how to manifest with the help of the whole Universe. Until then, I will continue to create a charming life with what I have and be clever with our income. I'm inspired by the story I told in the earlier chapter of Doreen. She and her daughters lived on loose change and government cheese for a few years, but it paid off. She worked hard in a lovely community college and earned two degrees quickly. She got a good job and lived well; she bought a cottage, always traveled, and went to concerts. She lived a great life. Being broke for a few years doesn't matter in the big scheme. When you are working toward something, you don't mind the sacrifices.

We won't always use the food bank, but I will always thrift and be a wise steward of the funds so we will live comfortably. And we don't mind the food bank. It is fun to bring home the vegetarian bags and get creative with what is in there. It's like those shows with the surprise chef box, where they have to create dishes with odd things in the box.

We have never felt poor in any way. Kids mustn't feel poor or ever feel the stress a parent may go through financially. They need their childhood, and they need to feel confident and secure. We have never experienced financial stress because we have always lived under our income, no matter how small; we have never had car payments, we bought cars with cash, and if we did have a credit card, it had a tiny limit, and we kept it paid off always. I used to get Amazon credit cards, but I don't do that anymore; ordering freely is just too tempting. We must wait until we've saved enough money to buy things. We have a Home Depot card, but we only use it if we have to, and we work overtime and extra to pay it off within a few months. We have always had affordable rents and mortgages. By affordable, I mean half our income or less, but without debt, it's doable without stress. Because I worshiped **The Complete Tightwad Gazette** and learned so much from all the frugal people out there, and I do everything I've learned, we have never had hard times.

I have so many good memories we would never have enjoyed if circumstances had been different. Suppose I hadn't chosen to stay home and be a homemaker, instead choosing to work and have plenty of money. There would have been more choices in where and what homes we purchased, but living in an upper-class neighborhood can be lonely. I've enjoyed most of our towns and always felt safe in our neighborhoods, even when the cops were weekly visitors at the slum apartments across the street. I've loved all the homes we have lived in for different reasons; the 860 sq. ft. house in the city was my favorite. I didn't care for the neighborhood; it was too suburban, and I looked out on the tan stucco side of our neighbor's house. But the house was delightful, and it was where I started my writing career. I loved the ranch house on the fruit farm, and we looked out every window at trees and orchards. The first house we owned was a sweet blue cottage, and I had almond trees, apple trees, kitchen gardens in the back yard, and a considerable tomato patch in the front yard that produced twenty quarts of spaghetti sauce the last year we lived there. This house, which I call Arthur, is my favorite. It is well-insulated; every window looks over the trees and our gardens. Even the big apartments across the way have charm. They are old and need painting, but there are giant, tall trees in a row blocking most of it across the street. We are on the side with the offices, a little shelter with mailboxes and the pool, and more trees. It looks more like a summer place where people come to vacation, and at night, they have warm streetlamps. The apartments are clean and quiet, and everyone works there. It is a hub of worker bees and friendly people.

All the time I've had with my children and all the warm meals, family visits, long walks to the rivers and through the forest, the movies we've watched, playing in the pool together, BBQing, and sitting out there reading. I love thinking about all these memories. Sometimes, just making a dish will bring back a warm memory of being with my kids. Not even doing anything special or laughing wildly, just being together and the house warm on a rainy day, having a delicious homemade meal in the works, or listening to a song on the radio.

Honestly, I may not have learned to cook so well and from scratch if we had plenty of money. I can be lazy. I love buying those bags of pot stickers, perogies, and frozen pizza. I love takeout. Papa Murphys, please make my pizza! But it was not within the budget, and we love fast food and takeout like any other person.

So, I learned how to make it. I learned how to make pizzas, hamburgers, Chinese food, Indian food, Taco Bell, pierogies, French fries, burritos, sushi, etc. Potstickers are on the list. Then I kept going back and forth between vegan and plant-based, so I had to relearn how to cook all the favorites but veganize them. That was the most fun and creative I've ever been in the kitchen. Those memories are my favorite of the first time I lasted a year being vegan, and I recreated everything vegan. I'm back to plant-based and cooking up a vegan storm again, and now I'm good at it. I know the best faux cheeses and vegan sour creams to work with or make. I know which faux meats to use or how to make them. That's another group of foods I've had to learn to make: plant-based meats, cheeses, milks, and eggs. It's all cheaper and tastes better.

Being frugal has forced me to be dynamic and creative, think outside the box, and do things I would have skipped if I had the funds.

Gardening. I love gardening and growing food, but that is another thing I wonder if I would have done if I wasn't trying to find ways to reduce our grocery bill. I love lush, tree-filled yards, but would I have put in the gardens and planted an orchard if I had lots of money and could buy all the produce I wanted for my family? We'll never know, and now I love to garden, so when there is more money, I'll still do it.

I wonder if we come into more wealth in the future, would I still cook from scratch and garden as much? Would I walk everywhere like I do? Would I read as much and try to educate myself as much? I feel the most inspired and driven now because I want to build my writing skills and make more money from my work. When money flows freely into our lives, it changes us. It can be for the good if we choose, but I have also seen people who became greedy, and the more they received, the more they wanted. It was never enough, and money became the focus, the passion, the drive...their whole reason for being. Then, there are the souls that become rich and they put the money into the community. All sorts of outstanding, life-giving projects to support animal and child well-being, reforesting projects, helping other countries learn better, healthier farming practices, and building schools and wells. Mr. Beast is a YouTuber with an enormous channel. He constantly puts vast wealth into projects to help people, forests, and villages. He uses his wealth and influence to do good things in this world. I feel that is why he keeps growing in success. You get what you give. Be generous, and abundance will come back to you.

We don't have much to share, but I will share as much as possible. I donate lovely books, furniture, clothes, and kitchen tools to the thrift store down the street or put them on the street like the rest of my neighbors. I take foods we don't eat, egg cartons, and bags to the food bank, and we volunteer in the Summer. I give the meat from the food bank to my neighbor, who is also on a tight budget. I donate small amounts to a few organizations I want to support, such as causes to protect animals or global reforesting projects. It isn't much, but we give where we can. As our orchards grow more extensive, we will one day have more than enough fruits and nuts to share, and I'll donate those to the food pantries. We have relied on the food pantries...or banks (I don't know the difference or if there is one) for a few seasons now. When my dear old friend was living with us, and an old carpenter was helping us rebuild one of the bathrooms, I had up to six people to feed, and I was grateful for the food pantry to stretch the groceries. I'm grateful now for our tiny grocery envelope.

Is this all temporary? Yes, it is. I believe in my soul that I will succeed more with my writing one day, and money will flow into our lives. Until then, I use resources for families like us, dig in the bag of frugal tricks, and hone my thrifty skills. In the meantime, I embrace this life because these may be our best years, not when we have wealth but now when we live humbly. When we do have wealth, I will probably donate most of it because I don't want to lose this precious lifestyle completely.

It is a beautiful life.

Now, we come to the end of our story. I hope I've inspired you. You don't have to be plant-based like me or do anything like me. Just take what sounded good and do that, or just enjoy this read.

The other day, I was visiting Craigslist. I check in daily, and someone posted, "Raid my bunker." I called the man, and Bali, and I went up the mountain with the truck and filled it to the top with bags of canned goods and mylar bags of grains, beans, and oats. It was insane. He had posted a few weeks ago, and I had ignored it, but I wanted to see what he had this time. We filled the back of the truck and the back seat. I spent two days sorting and filling my pantry and shelves in my closet that had remained empty. I needed a lot of shelves. I kept the vegetarian stuff and the Progresso soups because the kids like them. I had to create more shelves. I loaded over ten bags and dropped them off at the food bank today.

The man said he had a problem and was in recovery. I'm assuming he was a prepper, but then I realized that it was all fear- and stress-related and was letting it all go. Most cans were past the 'best by' date, but if they are undented, uncompromised, and unpunctured, they last for years, even a decade or more. I was thrilled by all the abundance and shared it with the community. I'm still feeling a little high from it. I can now create menus from this pantry for months. This saves us so much money, and we don't have to apply for CalFresh. We probably won't be using the food bank for a long time. I need creamers and fruits and vegetables every ten days to two weeks. Then our garden will start producing this summer. I can take a couple hundred a month and stock up on all that and coffee, along with little extras for vegan cooking.

This is just another example of how the Universe has our backs when we are working towards a new life, working well and smart, staying positive, and making good choices.

I will leave you with this thought. Paramhansa Yogananda wrote a Material Success Affirmation. There is a part that says, *"I lived in the thoughts of poverty and wrongly fancied I was poor, so I was poor. Now I am home, and thy consciousness has made me wealthy, made me rich."*

Wealth does not have to come in the form of money, but it helps to have enough to pay the bills and buy groceries to keep a roof over our heads. Wealth is being healthy and vibrant mentally and physically, having a few close relationships, a peaceful home, and living in a safe area. We can use our skills and imagination, our industriousness to make a good life out of what we have. Only we set limits on ourselves. The world and life are limitless. You have the whole Universe backing you. All it takes is learning to be positive, growing your inner happiness, and understanding that you deserve and can co-create any reality you choose. Faith without works is a biblical saying, and it is true. You must believe before you can see it and work toward it in mind, body, and soul.

Make your life cozy and love it.

Printed in Great Britain
by Amazon